T0319036

Chinese Jade

The Chinese people have honored, revered, and cherished jade for over 8,000 years. Consequently, jade has played a unique role in the development of Chinese culture. Jade carvings survive not simply as beautiful works of art, but also as important relics shedding light on the spiritual life of ancient China. Utilizing a wealth of archaeological evidence and illustrated with precious cultural artifacts, *Chinese Jade* provides an introduction to the fascinating world of Chinese jade from ancient to modern times.

Introductions to Chinese Culture

The thirty volumes in the Introductions to Chinese Culture series provide accessible overviews of particular aspects of Chinese culture written by a noted expert in the field concerned. The topics covered range from architecture to archaeology, from mythology and music to martial arts. Each volume is lavishly illustrated in full color and will appeal to students requiring an introductory survey of the subject, as well as to more general readers.

Yu Ming

CHINESE
JADE

CAMBRIDGE
UNIVERSITY PRESS

CAMBRIDGE
UNIVERSITY PRESS

University Printing House, Cambridge CB2 8BS, United Kingdom

One Liberty Plaza, 20th Floor, New York, NY 10006, USA

477 Williamstown Road, Port Melbourne, VIC 3207, Australia

314-321, 3rd Floor, Plot 3, Splendor Forum, Jasola District Centre, New Delhi - 110025, India

79 Anson Road, #06-04/06, Singapore 079906

Cambridge University Press is part of the University of Cambridge.

It furthers the University's mission by disseminating knowledge in the pursuit of education, learning and research at the highest international levels of excellence.

www.cambridge.org
Information on this title: www.cambridge.org/9780521186841

Originally published by China Intercontinental Press as
Chinese Jade (9787508513317) in 2009

© China Intercontinental Press 2009

This updated edition is published by Cambridge University Press with the permission of China Intercontinental Press under the China Book International programme 🦅.

For more information on the China Book International programme, please visit http://www.cbi.gov.cn/wisework/content/10005.html

Cambridge University Press retains copyright in its own contributions to this updated edition

© Cambridge University Press 2011

First published 2011

ISBN 978-0-521-18684-1 Paperback

Contents

Preface

The Chinese have respected, honored, revered, loved, and cherished jade for over 8,000 years. Chinese jade art, veiled in mystery and carrying spiritual sustenance, is rooted deeply in traditional Chinese culture and has played a role in Chinese social life like no other form of art.

As early as 6000BC, people began to use jade to make tools and ornaments. As primitive religions emerged in the Neolithic Age, jade artifacts gradually came to be regarded as gifts from the gods, and then became social status symbols in the Shang and Zhou dynasties when sacrificial rites developed. During the Han Dynasty, people turned to jade as a symbol of immortal life as a result of prevailing ideas about the existence of gods and the concept "deal with death just as with life." Although the art of jade-working experienced difficult times during the turbulent period of the Three Kingdoms to the Southern and Northern dynasties, jade art came back to life in the Tang, Song, Ming and Qing dynasties when, with peace restored in civil society, it provided spiritual sustenance for people and allowed them to express their inner feelings. Jade artifacts, integrating superb craftsmanship and carved according to the unique properties of the natural materials, resemble brilliant stars in traditional Chinese culture and shine in world history. The past 8,000 years have created a unique Chinese culture in which jade has been honored throughout the ages and the passion for jade has been incorporated into the heritage of the Chinese people. Jade culture is an integral part of the Chinese civilization, playing a unique and crucial role in cultural history.

CHINESE JADE

Picking Jade in the White Jade River by Song Yingxing (1587–1661), a scientist of the Ming Dynasty, in *The Exploitation of the Works of Nature*.

Unveiling the Mystery of Jade: An overview

Essence of Heaven and Earth—Jade

In simple terms, jade is the umbrella name for several specific minerals. In the eyes of the ancient Chinese, jade was a beautiful stone with a soft sheen, and jade wares are those carved from these minerals. As the jade wares made in various historical periods reflect different historical backgrounds and carry varying historical meanings, jade has both its natural and social attributes. The ancient people attributed the beauty of jade to its "five virtues." They compared the five properties of jade, for example, soft sheen, uniformity both inside and outside, sharp sound when struck, hard texture and strength, to the five virtues of people, namely benevolence, justice, wisdom, courage and purity, which are the social attributes of jade.

Thus jade was a beautiful stone in the eyes of the ancient people because its qualities coincided with the most-favored

Gilded green jade chimes, Qing Dynasty
Chimes were important musical instruments in the imperial court of the Qing Dynasty. Sixteen bells of the same shape and size constitute one set of chimes, and they produce high or low-pitched sounds when struck due to their different thicknesses, with the thinnest producing the lowest pitched sound.

aesthetic criteria. The ancestors of the Chinese nation compared jade with other stones for thousands of years before they could finally identify its distinctive features and recognize it easily, believing it to integrate the essence of the heaven and earth.

What are the features of beautiful jade?

Jade is beautiful in its qualities. Jade is tough and durable, so it is not easily broken. Slightly glossy and translucent, it displays an undefined beauty of feminine softness. With low thermal conductivity, it is less reactive to external heat and cold, and thus is suitable to be made into ornamental necklaces and small pieces of artwork one can hold in the hand. Because of its stable chemical attributes, jade is not easily corroded by acid and alkaline and, as a result, can remain underground uncorroded for millions of years.

The beauty of jade is also in its color. Multiple chemical elements result in the diverse colors of jade - as the ancient people said, "Some are as yellow as a steamed chestnut, some as white as grease and some as black as pure paint." Jade can also have colorful surfaces that look like pear skins, tiger skins or resemble other patterns. Jade wares of different colors display various senses of beauty and have varying functions.

Jade is beautiful in its sound. With its fine texture, jade can produce a sound that carries well when struck. The sound of jade musical stones, in particular, is melodious, pleasant, crisp and resonating. The "sound made by the knockings of gold and jade instruments," goes an old Chinese saying that described such a sound as the most beautiful in the world.

Jade is beautiful, but how can we identify such special stones?

Categories of jade vary. Different identification standards have been in place at different times, and this reflects the rich and profound connotation of Chinese jade culture. The materials used in jade working in all historical periods include: Hotan jade, jadeite, Xiuyan jade, Nanyang jade, lapis lazuli, turquoise, malachite, agate, crystal, amber and coral. Xinjiang Hotan jade and jadeite are the most important varieties.

Xinjiang Hotan jade, named after its place of origin, is a form of the mineral hornblende with hardness of 6–6.5 (Mohs scale). Jade falls into two categories: mountain material and seed material. The former is block-shaped and produced in the Kunlun Mountains, and the latter, rounded water-worn pebbles, usually with a red surface, are produced by White Jade River in Xinjiang. Hotan jade was the most-prized ancient Chinese material, and has such colors as white, yellow, grey, green and black. White jade is the most precious variety of Hotan jade, and the best of all is the "sheep-fat" white jade that is white, transparent, fine-textured and softly shiny. With only limited amounts available, "sheep-fat" jade is extremely expensive. Every dynasty since the Neolithic Age has particularly favored the creation of works made of Hotan jade for royalty and nobles, with a huge influence on Chinese jade culture.

With hardness of 6.5–7(Mohs scale), jadeite is a pyroxene

Hotan jade seed material with yellow surface.

mineral and mainly composed of aluminum sodium silicate. Transparent or translucent, it features such colors as green, white and red with glass-like sheen. Jadeite (*feicui*) was originally the name of birds. *Fei* is said to be the name of "red bird" and *cui* is the name of "green bird." Jadeite is also said to be a bird with red and green feathers, and the jade that has similar colors is called "jadeite." Jadeite that is pure, flawless, highly transparent

Raw emerald-green jadeite.

and very green is highly prized. According to an old Chinese saying "even immortals will find it hard to identify true jadeite." As the interior quality of jadeite cannot be judged by its outer appearances, those who, since ancient times, made or lost fortunes by speculating on the purity of jade have been too numerous to count. Burma is the major place of origin of jadeite. In China, jadeite works were most popular in the mid-Qing Dynasty (1644–1911). The appreciation of jade reached its peak in the late Qing Dynasty.

Carrier of Civilization—Jade Wares

Although jade is beautiful as a natural mineral, its beauty does not come solely from nature. Just as Emperor Taizong of Tang (r. 626–649) decreed, "Jade is beautiful in nature but will not be distinguished from common stones unless cut and chiseled by superior craftsmen." Jade can only embody cultural meanings and ambience and become the symbol of civilization when made into artifacts based on human aesthetic demands. "A piece of jade unless cut forms no article of virtue" - so goes a popular Chinese saying. Jade wares are those made of jade and cut following certain techniques and processes.

"A Stone from Other Hills May Serve to Polish the Jade of this One"

How are jade wares made? First an introduction to the tools used to make jade wares will be given, and then the production process will be described.

In different Chinese historical periods, jade-carving tools were very similar. The *tuoji*, also called *shuideng*, was the basic tool used to make jade ware. It is a grinding machine powered by a foot-treadle and grinders, known as *tuozi*, of different kinds and sizes, may be installed on its main axis. When two feet operate the treadle, the grinders rotate along the main axis. By adding quartz sand and water between the grinders and jade, artisans can grind and process the mineral. This kind of jade-working technique was recorded in *The Exploitation of the Works of Nature* written by Song Yingxing in the Ming Dynasty: "Use smelted iron as the disc and a basin to contain the sand when cutting jade. Add sand while pedaling to rotate the disc, then the jade will be cut gradually." Another implement used in grinding is the *zhatuo,* which is equivalent to the grinding wheel saw in modern industry and is made of iron. However, the hardness of iron is about 5 (Mohs scale), but that of jade is 6–7, so the iron *zhatuo* is unable to cut jade. Only when quartz sand, with hardness of 7 and above, is added is it possible to grind jade. Jade-working in ancient times was accomplished by relying on grinding sand. "A stone from other hills may serve

The Exploitation of the Works of Nature: A comprehensive work on science and technology written by Song Yingxing, a scientist in the Ming Dynasty. It records a wide array of ancient Chinese technologies. It comprises three volumes that were further divided into eighteen chapters and includes 121 illustrations that describe the names, shapes and working procedures of more than 130 production technologies and tools. Western scholars, including Joseph Needham, have stressed the immense historical value of Song's work.

Making jade with *zhatuo*.

to polish the jade of this one," advises a famous Chinese saying revealing the key to jade working. Superior jade wares, rather than carved, were ground mainly by "stones from other hills," in other words jade-grinding sand, supplemented with water. With social development and technology, modern jade ware processing has changed a lot. Nowadays, electric tools with carborundum discs are used, and jade-grinding sand is directly incorporated in the grinding wheels, which have a hardness of more than 7 and are capable of processing jade directly.

It is now time to look at how jade ware is processed. The major processes include material selection, design, coarse carving, fine carving and polishing.

Jade artifacts are made depending on the nature of the material available. What a piece of jade is most suitable to be carved into

Processing jade with grinding sand.

depends on its shape, color and flaws. Generally speaking, it is better to choose flawless and large specimens of jade for large artifacts and smaller specimens for smaller ornaments. Jade with flesh tones may be used for exquisite carvings. Design may start once the jade is selected.

Design is crucial to making jade artifacts. Typically, designers will develop ideas for carvings based on the colors, size, texture and shape of the jade. First, jade will be used to the maximum extent to avoid unnecessary waste; second, the color will be cleverly used to produce the best effect; third, jade cracks and flaws will be hidden following the principle of "making best use of the advantages and bypassing the disadvantages." The initial design for jade ware may be put on paper or drawn directly on to the jade. Coarse carving begins after the design is finished.

Exquisite carving: By using the natural colors and textures of jade and suitable carving techniques, carvings demonstrate a unique form of jade craftsmanship, which cleverly combines shapes and colors to render perfect artistic effects. With innovative shapes and bright colors, carving integrated all the jade techniques and art of ancient China.

Coarse carving refers to carving out rough outlines based on the requirements of the design. The major processes involved are rough cutting of the jade, and removing of excess material outside the design lines to shape the basic outline. In this process, cracks inside the jade are avoided as much as possible to make it perfect. Coarse carving is vital to the success of the whole process of jade working.

Special techniques are needed in coarse carving. These include enchasing, openwork, relief and carving in the round Enchasing means to engrave patterns at different depths on the jade surface; the patterns are relatively deep but do not pierce the jade ware. Openwork entails piercing the jade surface and carving seemingly transparent patterns. Relief, including high relief and bas-relief, refers to engraving different shapes on

After it was selected, jade would first be cut, then came the designing and coarse carving.

the jade surface. Figures, animals, flowers, vases and furnaces carved in the round are all complete and solid forms. Refined carving follows coarse carving.

Refined carving, as the name implies, must be performed with great care. It includes elaborate carving and decoration. In the process of refined carving, the outline of jade will be further detailed to make the final designs, which can be as diverse as flowers, birds and beasts as well as human figures, mountains and rivers, and as true, dynamic and expressive as possible. Whereas bigger cutting tools are adopted in coarse carving, smaller grinding tools are used in fine carving. The parts that are finest and most difficult to carve are fashioned in the final step of the carving process. Polishing follows fine carving.

Polishing, actually a simple kind of fine grinding, is about polishing the jade surface with special tools and fine, hard polishing powder, to help remove coarse marks on the jade surface and make the surface bright and smooth.

Polishing is crucial in jade working. No fine carving alone can make a coarse jade surface become smooth and show the

Refined carving.

beautiful effect typical of crystal jade. Only perfect polishing can help display the soft sheen and elegance of jade and further manifest the noble qualities of jade ware.

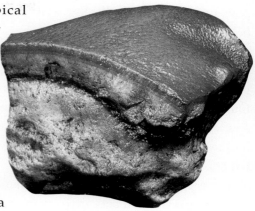

Braised pork-shaped jade carving, Qing Dynasty Currently in the Palace Museum in Taipei. The artwork, exquisite and vivid, incorporates ingenious use of color and displays superb craftsmanship.

Thus, a piece of raw jade becomes a jade artifact after the above processes. It not only incorporates the designers' artistic inspiration and the superior carving skills of jade carvers, but also bears cultural information about society and signs of the times.

Rich Categories and Wide-ranging Purposes

The Chinese have a unique passion for jade, having created numerous jade works in diverse categories, with rich forms and wide-ranging purposes. Jade ware may be roughly classified into the following categories:

Ritual jade ware refers to those artifacts used by ancient people in sacrifices and other ceremonies. The Chinese nation has a long history of rites and ceremonies, and offering sacrifices to heaven and ancestors was an important rite in ancient times. Jade used in these ceremonies included such sacrificial wares as *bi, cong, gui, zhang, hu* and *huang*.

Hierarchy jade was used by rulers of all dynasties to distinguish social status. Chinese jade had been imbued with power since the time of the first dynasty. Hierarchy jade included belt ornaments and palace beads.

Funerary jade was used by ancient people for preserving bodies. In Chinese history, when burying bodies, jade was believed to make both bodies and souls immortal and even to help souls enter heaven and gain a new life. Funeral jade mainly included clothes, *sai*, *han* and *wo* (jade items placed in the corpse's mouths and hands).

To the present day, people wear ornamental jade. The first Chinese jade artifacts were ornamental. Ornamental jade includes hairpins, earrings, rings, necklaces and belt hooks.

Utilitarian jade was for everyday use. To enjoy a luxurious life, the noble and rich in Chinese history usually had jade processed into wares with practical functions. They include such craftsmen's tools as axes, knives, shovels and adzes, items used in writing like brush pots, brush washers, paper weights, and seal boxes, as well as incense burners, bottles, bowls and kettles.

Decorative jade was for enjoyment. Royalty, nobility, rich businessmen and scholars liked to place jade artwork on shelves or desks to show off wealth or sophistication. Commonly seen decorative items included *shanzis* and *ruyis*, as well as carved animals, plants and figures.

There is also some special jade ware including religious artifacts, archaized jade and exotic jade. Chinese jade has been

Bi: A disc-like jade with a central circular hole. **Cong**: A hollow jade carving, square on the outside and cylindrical inside. **Gui**: A sort of plate-shaped jade with the bottom being flat and straight and the upper part being triangle-shaped or straight. **Zhang**: A belt shaped jade with the bottom being flat and straight and the upper part being knife-edged on one side. It is also described as "zhang combining half of a gui" because it looks like a half gui. **Hu**: A tiger-shaped jade ware made by round carving or tiger-shaped pattern jade carvings. **Huang**: An arc-shaped jade carving. It is also described as "huang combining half of a bi" because it looks like part of the bi.

Jade *sai*: Also called "*juiqiao sai*" (jade used to block a corpse's nine orifices). The "nine orifices" referred to two eyes, two earholes, two nostrils, the mouth, genitalia and anus. The Han people believed that the nine orifices could release energy like gas, and once the energy was used up, the body would decay. Thus they use jade to preserve human energy.
Jade *han*: Also called "*hanyu*," was a type of funeral jade placed inside a corpse's mouth. Different from the "*kousai*" (one of the *juiqiao sai*) that was placed in the mouth, jade *hans* were mostly cicada-shaped.
Jade *wo*: Was a jade artifact placed in the deads' hands, reflecting the idea that the ancient Chinese could not bear to see the dead leave the world empty-handed.

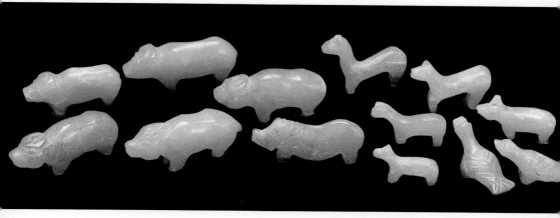

Jade han (jade put in the mouth of the dead for burial), the Warring States Period
Twenty-one pieces of jade *han* were unearthed from the tomb of the Marquis Yi of the State
of Zeng, located in Suizhou, Hubei. Small in size, they are in the shapes of dogs, bulls,
goats, pigs and ducks.

involved in a wide range of aspects of Chinese culture, from
politics, religion and morality to life and art.

Colorful Decorative Patterns and Magnificent Decorations

Decorative patterns were often carved on the jade surface. For
the ancient Chinese, jade had both aesthetic and psychological
functions, often used as a talisman to ward off evil spirits or to
bring good luck. This further enhanced the development of jade
decoration. The origins of such patterns were related to either
nature or the gods. Some were closely associated with people's
lives, including patterns that were grain-shaped or resembled
germinating seeds, protruding round shapes resembling nipples,
and patterns resembling rush mats. Some decorative patterns
were related to natural phenomena, such as cloud and bird
patterns. Others were those of imaginary animals created by
ancient humans. For example, the dragon, a combination of a

Octagonal jade cup with honeysuckle patterns, Tang Dynasty
White and crystal, this is an octagonal and elliptical-shaped cup with its outer surface featuring honeysuckle patterns.

fierce animal's head and snake's body, was later developed into one incorporating such elements as antlers, shrimp eyes, fish scales and eagle claws to form typical mythical totem images. The glutton pattern described a greedy and ferocious beast that was one of the nine sons of the dragon. The hornless dragon pattern described a gecko-like monster in ancient folklore that could be found in forests. These imaginary beasts all reflected the spiritual consciousness of the minds of the ancient Chinese people.

Patterns with Auspicious Meanings

The Chinese, who have a unique passion for jade, typically make them into symbols of virtues, rituals, power and luck. Most Chinese jade artifacts have patterns with auspicious meanings. Such patterns involved wide-ranging themes and were developed into relatively fixed figurative symbols.

Jade saucer with double hornless dragon design, Ming Dynasty

For example, dragons, phoenixes, elephants and goats were auspicious signs and were incorporated into such sayings as "Dragon and Phoenix Showing Auspices," "Elephants Bringing Peace," "Three Goats Bringing Good Luck," and so on. Peonies, lotuses, crab apples, apples, roosters and persimmons symbolized wealth and were incorporated into such ideas as "Wealth and prosperity fill the hall," "Richness, nobility and peace," and "Glory all one's life." In Chinese the words for bats, bergamots and kettles are homonyms for plentiful blessings and represented in such expressions as "Blessings descend from the sky," "Five blessings in a row," and "Great happiness." Monkeys, fishes, roosters and ducks implied fame and fortune and were displayed in sayings like "Monkey on the horse," "Carp jumping over the dragon gate," and "Five sons in glory." Pines, cypresses, peaches, tortoises and cranes symbolized immortal life and were incorporated into ideas like "Living as long as the tortoise and the crane," "Pine and crane," and "Presenting fat peaches for birthday celebrations." Badgers, magpies and spiders implied festive occasions and were shown in such patterns as "Happy together," "Joys expressed on brows," and "Happiness comes from heaven."

From generation to generation, the Chinese have expressed their hopes through such concepts and characters.

Fruit of Chinese Civilization—Chinese Jade Culture

Chinese jade is a cultural phenomenon that reflects both material and spiritual culture. Jade culture runs through the whole history of Chinese civilization. It has its origins in the early Neolithic Age, continued in the middle and late periods of the Neolithic Age, and developed through each early society. Jade penetrated every aspect of social life and took root in the minds of all the Chinese people.

Jade was the Medium between Humans and the Gods

In antiquity, when nature worship prevailed, people felt awed by magnificent and rare jade, but were unable to identify its true origin. Jade was therefore considered to be something magical that integrated the souls of heaven and earth, as well as mountains and rivers. As Confucius said: "Jade is the essence of mountains." In the eyes of the ancient people, jade was a gift from the gods and should have magical properties; hence jade was believed to be endowed with fantastic powers.

In ancient China, people tended to resort to the blessings of the gods when faced with uncertainties of nature or fortunes or misfortunes in life. Thus, jade ware was considered to be the medium used to connect humans with the gods, to ward off evil spirits, and pray for good luck. Desires were expressed through the patterns and auspicious words carved on jade, such as *changle* ("forever happiness") jade in the Eastern Han Dynasty and "Having both happiness and longevity" pendants in the Ming and Qing dynasties. Meanwhile, jade artifacts were also used to protect their owners from evil spirits and disasters; the "evil oppression" jade pendants were a case in point.

"Changle" (eternal happiness) jade *bi*, Eastern Han Dynasty Featuring "changle" in *zuan* script and double hornless dragons on the upper part of its surface, it is currently in the Palace Museum collection in Beijing. The jade *bi* was once deeply loved and cherished by the Emperor Qianlong and had long been used for decoration in the imperial court.

Jade was the Symbol of Power and Status

The concept of jade representing power and status appeared in the late Neolithic Age, which showed the shaping of social differentiation and ruling cliques that exercised political, military and religious power. Since the Zhou Dynasty (1046–256 BC), rulers had many jade ritual wares and ornaments to serve as symbols of power, safeguarding their feudal ritual system. Ancient literature like the *Rites of the Zhou Dynasty* detailed the names, forms, specifications and purposes of jade ware which symbolized hierarchies in the Zhou Dynasty, demonstrating the rigid, complex system of jade use. Later dynasties in Chinese history all specified strictly the proper ritual ware and jade ornaments for people of different social status to avoid confusion and transgression of boundaries. Examples include the belts used since the Tang Dynasty (618–907), and quills and palace beads. Only emperors could use pure jade. Those at lower levels of society were only permitted to use inferior jade that was equivalent to their social status.

Jade was the Symbol of Virtue and Conduct

In ancient times, the natural qualities of jade were closely related to views about good and evil, right and wrong, honor and disgrace, as well as beauty and ugliness, and served as criteria used to assess and judge human conduct.

Jade group pendant, Western Zhou Dynasty
Unearthed from the tomb of a Marquis in the State of Jin in Quwo County, Shanxi Province, it consists of 282 pieces of jade in different shapes.

This led to the development of the concept of "A gentleman comparing virtue to a gem," and the doctrine of "virtue of jade" that became widespread, with lasting effect and deep impact in Chinese jade cultural history. This helped the idea of the "beauty of jade" develop into the "beauty of humans."

The doctrine "virtue of jade" stated "jade is the necessity of a gentleman," and "a gentleman always carries a jade pendant." Endowed with rich moral properties, jade best embodied virtue

Carrying jade symbolised the virtues of a gentleman in ancient times.

and conduct, and thus became the symbol of the virtuous gentleman. When these men carried jade pendants, they would knock together to produce a melodious and pleasant sound; the gentleman who carried them was required to walk in a graceful manner and behave with virtuous values. Thus, carrying jade became a symbol of honesty and of honorable gentlemen.

Jade as a Token of Wealth

In Chinese culture, jade is considered a treasure of the world. It is the most beautiful thing that is capable of communicating with the gods and serving as a symbol of good virtue and conduct. Since ancient times, jade has been passed from generation to generation as national treasures and family heirlooms. Since the Qin Dynasty (221–206 BC), when the imperial jade seal was carved using priceless *Heshi* jade, emperors of all dynasties had seals made of jade to represent imperial power. A family of great wealth is typically described as "the hall is filled with gold and jade." Author Cao Xueqin also used this metaphor to describe the Jia family in *The Dream of the Red Chamber*, one of the four great classical Chinese novels: "The Jia family is so rich that it even has halls carved from white jade and horses wrought from gold," indicating the family's great wealth. Jade as a token of wealth was manifested to its greatest value in the Qing Dynasty (1644–1911), and this was discussed in *A Guide to Antiques* by Zhao Ruzhen, published in 1942, "There are no figures in the middle or upper class in the capital that do not carry jade. They carry jade for recreation at home and as the token of wealth outside. Jade will inevitably be shown off when friends meet each other and be the major topic of conversation on such occasions as gatherings or talks. Any families without jade are not the mansions of scholar-officials and any clothes without jade are not complete; it seems improper for those not carrying jade to join in a friends' gathering, and also for those lacking in knowledge of jade to participate in friends' discussions. Jade is so important that all social figures spare no effort to pursue it." So, the material value of jade became the criterion measuring the wealth and sophistication of upper class families.

In *The Dream of the Red Chamber*, "white-jade halls and gold horses" were used to describe the wealth of the Jia family.

The Dream of the Red Chamber Embodies Chinese Jade Culture

In *The Dream of the Red Chamber*, also known as *The Story of the Stone*, one of the greatest Chinese novels, Jia Baoyu, the main character,

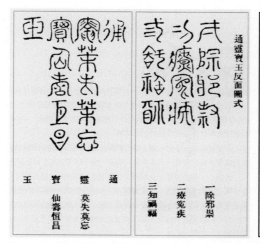

Patterns on both sides of the "Precious Jade of Tongling" described in *The Dream of the Red Chamber.*

was born with a piece of jade in his mouth. This stone remains the theme throughout the twists and turns of this moving story. The "Precious Jade of Tongling" connects all parts of the plot and its influence on the luck of Jia Baoyu is regarded as a miniature portrait of the "Grand View Garden," the setting for much of the story. Intact jade represents life and broken jade represents death. Jade becomes the symbol of Baoyu's individual honor and disgrace, as well as the rise and fall of the family. On the obverse side of the jade there are eight inscribed characters, "Mo shi mo wang, xian shou heng chang" ("You will have longevity and wealth as long as you do not lose or forget the jade") as well as the four characters "Tong ling bao yu" ("Precious Jade of Tongling"). On the reverse side are twleve characters "Yi chu xie sui, er liao yuan ji, san zhi huo fu" ("First, it can ward off the evil spirits; second, it can treat diseases; third, it can foretell fortunes and misfortunes"). These words inscribed on the jade show that it is a pendant combining both good wishes and protection from evil spirits. The traditional Chinese legend "Nu Wa

Patching up the Sky" is also adopted to foreshadow the Precious Jade of Tongling, which makes the story more complete and incorporates Chinese jade culture into the plot of the novel. *The Dream of the Red Chamber* embodies the author's knowledge of jade and reflects ancient people's understanding of jade culture, representing this culture through literature.

Jade culture has developed continuously throughout the 8,000 years of Chinese civilization that has stretched from the Neolithic Age to today. The evolution of Chinese jade ware falls into four general stages: jade for the gods during the Neolithic Age; jade for rulers during the Xia and Shang dynasties to the Han Dynasty; jade for the people from the Sui and Tang dynasties to Ming and Qing dynasties; and modern times when traditional jade culture has been inherited and carried forward.

Footprint in the World of Sacred Gods: The Time of Jade for the Gods

CHINESE JADE

T he Neolithic Age dates to 10,000 to 4,000 years ago. In the middle and late Neolithic Age, jade was used to make ritual objects. Because there were no scientific means to understand natural and social phenomena at that time, early worship of gods developed and gradually led to sacrificial rituals performed by designated people using special tools. In the Neolithic Age, jade was the most important form of ritual ware used to connect humans with the gods. As a result, this period was known as "the time of jade for the gods."

Skull with the right eye-socket embedded with a jade ring, Xinglongwa Culture Unearthed from Chamber No. 4 of a tomb at the Xinglonggou site located in Aohan Banner, Inner Mongolia, the jade ring was embedded inside the right eye socket of the corpse to serve as his eye.

The earliest jade artifacts discovered so far are those from the Xinglongwa Culture, which indicates that Chinese jade ware and jade culture were initially shaped in the early Neolithic Age around 8,000 years ago. Later, jade culture extended into all parts of the vast Chinese lands and flourished. The jade ware culture of the Neolithic Age, having begun with the Xinglongwa Culture, ended with the Longshan Culture. Outstanding pieces from this period are known from the Xinglongwa and Hongshan Cultures of the Liaohe River area in northeastern China, from the Lingjiatan Culture in the Yangtze-Huaihe area, the Qijia Culture in the upper reaches of the Yellow River in northwest China, the Shijiahe and Liangzhu Cultures in the middle and lower reaches of the Yangtze River, as well as from the Longshan Culture that spread across China.

Jade Ware of Xinglongwa Culture

The Xinglongwa Culture that emerged in Northeast China's Liaohe area around 6000BC was named after the Xinglongwa site located in the Aohan banner of Chifeng, Inner Mongolia, and is regarded as the source of Chinese jade culture.

Why is the jade ware of Xinglongwa Culture given such an important position in the history of Chinese jade? Objectively speaking, the area offered abundant jade materials and this enabled the people to distinguish jade from commonplace stones. Also, people at that time boasted relatively advanced stone-working techniques that could also be applied in jade processing. These features were the basis for the presence of jade culture. Jade ware was small in size and variety; and jade earrings were the most common form of objects during this period (see below).

Jade rings, Xinglongwa Culture
This picture shows a pair of yellow-green jade rings. Circular with a slit, these rings were ritual items in the period of the Xinglongwa Culture.

The unique aesthetic concepts of the Xinglongwa people were the subjective reasons why the area was the source of jade culture. Jade ware was used for social purposes at that time. Prior to that, jade-working tools unearthed from some sites of the Paleolithic Age showed no essential differences from other stone tools, as they were simply for practical use. As a result, jade in the Paleolithic Age was still used in the same way as other stones and not separated from the latter. The presence of jade ware was an individual, accidental phenomenon rather than a common, purposeful social practice; it was not possible for jade to embody features of society at that time. Jade ware of the Xinglongwa Culture was different. Its purposes were separated from utilitarian ware and the more advanced use of jade appeared to help shape a relatively standard system of use. For instance, jade earrings, one of the main jade artifacts, were circular with a narrow

Human face-shaped jade ornament, Xinglongwa Culture
This piece is yellow-brown and elliptical. The two arc grooves on the left and right sides were embedded with triangular-shaped mussel shells, which represent the mouth and teeth. This ornament might be the image of a god as imagined by the people of the Xinglongwa Culture.

slit on the rim designed to clip onto the earlobe of a woman. Yet though earrings might initially be ornaments for women, they also seem to have served as special tools to connect humans with the gods.

A pair of earrings was unearthed from the Xinglonggou site in Chifeng, Inner Mongolia, one of the settlements in the middle period of Xinglongwa Culture. The earrings were found beside the two ears of the corpse, suggesting the use of jade earrings that clipped on the earlobes. As matrilineal society was the dominant social form in the Xinglongwa Culture period, females were both rulers and those in charge of communicating with the gods, and it is thought that the jade earrings were the tools they used to connect themselves with heaven. When the tribes experienced great events that required significant action, jade earrings were thought to help them hear voices from heaven and make corresponding decisions. The jade wares of the Xinglongwa Culture were therefore more than simple ornaments, though they were worn for beauty. They were also endowed with social and cultural meaning and became the medium connecting humans with the gods. The fact that ancient people actively sought jade and distinguished it from other stones to make artifacts that carried their spiritual and cultural ideas marked a new concept in using jade and helped shape the attributes of Chinese jade ware.

The jade ware of Xinglongwa Culture marked the start of the glorious history of Chinese jade ware, and also laid a solid foundation for the prehistoric northern jade ware center represented by the Hongshan Culture.

Jade Ware of Hongshan Culture

Hongshan Culture, a representative of the Neolithic Age, some 5,000 to 6,000 years ago, derived its name from the Hongshan site in Chifeng, Inner Mongolia. The period of the Hongshan Culture saw relatively developed religious activities and jade ware during this period featured art dominated by animals, made by carving in the round, which were used in religious rituals.

The jade ware of the Hongshan Culture played a crucial role in the progress of Chinese civilization. With the increasing number of clan tribes, there was an urgent need to unite the scattered forces within the tribes, and such cohesion was achieved mainly through sacrificial activities paying respects to heaven and the ancestors. Jade ware of the Hongshan Culture helped connect humans with heaven and their ancestors at sacrificial ceremonies. Combined with primitive beliefs and totem worship, jade artifacts at the time were shaped into birds, pigs, dragons and tortoises that were stitched on shamans' robes to be worn when such major events as foreign invasion or sudden natural calamities occurred. At that point, the shamans began to pray, communicating with the gods and ancestors and listening to their orders, and the jade artifacts on their robes became the ties linking the gods, ancestors and humans. Those who owned jade ware had the privilege of communicating with the gods, which further transformed the great power of conveying orders of the gods and deciding the fate of tribes. People in the Hongshan period devoted much effort to jade working as they considered jade extremely sacred, helping the tribes face wars and disasters. This helped promote the integration of tribes and development of a civilized society. Jade ware of Hongshan Culture, therefore, can in some ways be seen as a catalyst for human civilization.

Most of the jade materials in this period were tremolites that were mainly produced in jade mines in Xiyugou, Xiuyan of Liaoning.

Jade figurine, Hongshan Culture
This jade figurine is light green, with both legs together, two arms bent in front of his chest and his back hunched. It has a bobbed hairstyle, a round face and strong facial features. The carving lines are short and rough. It might be an ancestral god worshipped by the people in the period of Hongshan Culture.

Jade pig-dragon, Hongshan Culture
Made of light green jade mixed with brown spots, the pig-dragon has a relatively large head and a circular twisting body. With two round eyes slightly protruding outward, it also has a hole in its neck.

CHINESE JADE

Although jade outcrops were mostly found at the tops of mountains, exploitation of the resources was not easy job and required advanced techniques. Primitive people first found cracks in jade mineral deposits, inserted a piece of wood and lit it, then cooled the wood with water when it was heated to a high temperature. This process, known as thermal expansion and contraction, made jade materials split, so they could be extracted. Though primitive, the process was very effective.

Tremolites: metamorphic rocks produced mixing and deposition of dolomites and quartz, with crystals appearing to be radiating or in columnar arrays.

Dragons, pig-dragons, birds and cloud-shaped pendants made of jade were unearthed in a number of areas from the Hongshan Culture, with shapes and styles that were amazingly similar. Take the jade pig-dragons, for example. Though more than ten pieces of the jade ware were unearthed from different areas, thousands of kilometers apart, surprisingly they had basically the same shape. Although different in size, they all had pig heads: big ears, round eyes, twisting bodies and tiny holes on the back. This was almost the same with other items, which suggested that jade ware made at that time followed a certain set of rules. For example, in the Hongshan Culture period, rigid requirements were imposed

Cloud-shaped jade pendant, Hongshan Culture
Measuring 28.6 cm long, 9.5 cm wide and 0.6 cm thick, this pendant is the largest jade ware surviving from the Hongshan Culture. It renders a serious and mysterious effect in both weight and size and was a piece of sacrificial jade.

on the shapes and patterns of jade artifacts that were designed to link humans with heaven. Two possibilities might account for the similarity of shapes: (i) All jade ware was made by one of the tribes and passed onto other tribes via trade and exchange; (ii) the result of mutual exchange of jade ware made by different tribes.

Jade ware was so precious in this period that the ultimate treatment for the dead was to bury them with jade ware, rather than using other materials. This was the phenomenon of "exclusive interment of jade" typical of Hongshan Culture. The number of buried jade artifacts also represented the social status of the tomb occupant. Pit No.5 at the Niuheliang site in Jianping County of Liaoning was a typical tomb of "exclusive interment of jade" from Hongshan Culture. The tomb occupant was a man, with two big jade rings on both sides of his head, a cloud-shaped jade pendant and a flat-bottomed cylindrical ornament with an oblique opening in front of his chest, a jade bracelet around his left wrist and one jade tortoise in each hand. These jade pieces must have been sacrificial artifacts he often used when he was alive, and he was thought to be a tribal head or a great shamen. Given his high social status and great power, only jade was chosen to accompany him after his death, and this also showed the important role of jade.

The jade dragon is the most precious item surviving from Hongshan Culture. The dragon, the symbol of the Chinese nation, has been a god worshipped by the Chinese for thousands of years. In ancient folklore, the dragon was the god in charge of clouds and rain and one of the most powerful and influential gods. As ancient people longed for favorable weather and great harvests, they would leave no stone unturned to offer sacrifices to the dragon god.

The discovery of the jade dragon from Hongshan Culture was accidental. South of one of the mountains that lie to the north of

A typical example of "exclusive interment of jade" unearthed from the site of Niuheliang in Jiaping County, Liaoning Province.

a village named Sanxingtala, Wengniute banner, Chifeng, Inner Mongolia, is a vast stretch of hilly land. On a spring day in 1971, local villagers came to plant trees. The shovel of a peasant who was digging the soil touched something hard. It was a piece of jade ware, but the peasant did not realize its value and gave it to his children as a toy to play with. When the local authority of cultural heritage was informed of this find, the dragon was sent to the State Cultural Heritage Department. This was the earliest Chinese jade dragon to be discovered. The 26-cm-tall dragon is made of a complete piece of green Xiuyan jade carved in the

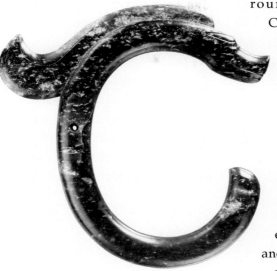

Jade pig-dragon, Hongshan Culture

round. With a twisting C-shaped body and a mane on its back, the dragon has a long head, tightly closed mouth extending forward and turning slightly up, its nose has a flat front end and two symmetrical round nostrils, it has two shuttle-shaped eyes, and its forehead and jaw are both marked with fine grid patterns. All these features make it appear powerful and energetic. With all parts in perfect harmony, the extraordinary jade dragon reflects the awe the people of the Hongshan Culture felt towards the mythical animal. Its primitive style and unsophisticated carving techniques are of great historical value, and it is thus called "China's No.1 Dragon."

Jade wares of Hongshan Culture boasted profound meaning and reflected the social, spiritual phenomena of that time. As a period with an extremely brilliant jade culture, Hongshan Culture laid a foundation for later Chinese jade culture.

Jade Ware of Lingjiatan Culture

The Lingjiatan Culture, a branch of the Neolithic Age culture in South China's Yangtze-Huaihe area, was named after the

Lingjiatan site in Tongzha Town, Hanshan County, Anhui
Province. Existing about 5,500–5,300 years ago, it was similar to
the Hongshan Culture situated in the northern areas.

Among all prehistoric jade ware, those of Lingjiatan
Culture had the richest variety of styles, as well as the most
representative figurines, dragons, tortoises, carved rectangular
plates, flat-bottomed cylindrical ornaments with oblique
openings and trumpet-shaped ornaments made of jade. The
numerous shapes and styles enriched and advanced the
evolution of Chinese jade. One particularly notable artifact is a
jade pig weighing 76 kg.

Standing jade figurine, Lingjiatan Culture
Made of grey-white jade, this jade figurine might be an ancestral god worshipped by the
people in the period of Lingjiatan Culture.

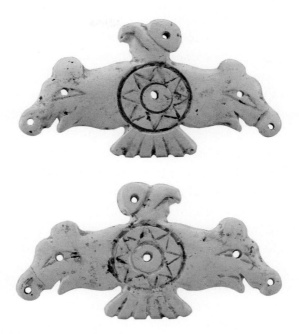

Eagle-shaped jade pendant, Lingjiatan Culture
Carved from grey-white jade, the eagle extends both wings and looks to one side, with two eyes represented by holes. With a pig's head carved on each side of the wings, the bird is decorated with a circle with octagon star patterns. Its tail is carved in detail with fan-shaped indented patterns.

Jade ware of Lingjiatan Culture was made with very advanced tools that included *tuoju* tools specifically made for hard materials like agate, as these thin and sharp tools are ideal for pattern carving. Techniques such as intaglio, relief, round carving and openwork, as well as cutting, drilling and polishing techniques had all reached a very high level in this period. Exquisite Lingjiatan jade wares were mainly those of small sizes. The jade trumpet ornament is an ideal example; it was regular in shape and carefully processed, with the diameter of the tiniest hole being 0.1 cm and approaching the rim of ware, showing the finest workmanship.

The jade ware of the Lingjiatan Culture, with its varied shapes and diverse styles, embodied rich cultural connotations. Like the jade ware of the Hongshan Culture, those of Lingjiatan also had the connotation of the primitive culture that prevailed in the Neolithic Age, when activities to predict the future were frequent in daily life. Jade ware such as carved rectangular plates, tortoises, eagles, dragons and figurines, with innovative shapes and mysterious meanings, conveyed messages involving primitive Eight Diagrams, sun worship, early astronomy as well as rites, rituals, funeral customs and civilization, and vividly display the social life of that time. Jade ware of Lingjiatan represented another peak in prehistoric jade use.

This jade flat-bottomed cylindrical ornament with an oblique mouth was a fortune-telling tool unearthed from the Lingjiatan Culture site in 2007. Although some flat-bottomed cylindrical ornaments with an oblique mouth have also been unearthed from Hongshan Culture sites, and have been described as crown-like ornaments, their purpose remained unknown until the discovery at the Lingjiatan site. This object still contained

Flat-bottomed cylindrical jade ornament with an oblique opening, Lingjiatan Culture.

Rectangular-shaped jade ornament with carved patterns, Lingjiatan Culture

jade fortune lots when unearthed, revealing its purpose as a fortune-telling tool used by shamens. This was the first discovery to confirm the continuity of Chinese civilization for 5,000 years. Even today, it is still possible to draw a lot from a fortune-telling container in the hope of praying for peace in some Chinese temples. This is very similar to the scene some 5,000 years ago, with the difference being that modern people draw lots just for fun, while in the worshipful atmosphere back then, shamens in robes drew lots to determine the fate of tribes. Though great changes have taken place in the world, Chinese culture remains the same as before.

A jade-carved rectangle plate, another piece of artwork of Lingjiatan Culture, has an important astronomical meaning. Round holes were drilled on each of the four sides of the jade plate, with two concentric circles carved in the center. In the smaller circle is a square pattern with an outer octagon. Between the two circles were radial arrows, and between the larger circle and the four corners were four arrow-like patterns. In ancient astronomy, the large circle represented changes of the universe and seasons. Just as the *Xici* chapter in *Zhouyi* (*The Book of Changes*) said, "The universe was first in a chaotic state called *Taiji*, or *Tianyi*, which generated two *Yis*. Then the two *Yis* generated four *Xiangs* that further generated the Eight Trigrams." Here, the *Taiji*, or *Tianyi*, refers to the North Pole in the astronomical calendar that was endowed with a supreme position by the ancient people. The two *Yis* refer to heaven and earth that were also called *Yin* (earth) and *Yang* (heaven). Given the theory of "Round Heaven and Square Earth" mentioned in the ancient books, the circles on the jade plate probably symbolized heaven and the square pattern earth. The four crossed lines and eight angles in the center of the jade plate, as well as the eight arrows and four arrows coincide with the concepts of four *Xiangs* and Eight Diagrams mentioned in Zhouyi and the theory of "Round Heaven and Square Earth." Furthermore, the four *Xiangs* and Eight Diagrams relate to ancient Chinese seasons, equaling the "four seasons and eight festivals" in the Chinese lunar calendar. Therefore, it can be concluded that the patterns on the jade plate were most likely an intuitive description of astronomy and geography by the primitive people in Lingjiatan, and this also proved the presence of a Chinese calendar as early as 5,000 years ago.

Jade ware constituted the most wonderful part of Lingjiatan Culture. Jade ware with its soft sheen did more than entertain the gods and enrich lives of nobility; they were objects longed for and pursued by the vast numbers of ordinary people. Jade ware buried together with figures of great power and wealth numbered hundreds of pieces, showing how the whole of society valued jade in the Lingjiatan Culture period. This was a peak in the time of jade for the gods.

Jade Ware of Liangzhu Culture

The Liangzhu Culture was a branch of the Neolithic Age culture in the Taihu Lake areas in the lower reaches of the Yangtze River. Existing about 5,000 to 4,500 years ago, it was named after the Liangzhu site located in Hangzhou, Zhejiang Province. As an art form dominated by geometric shapes, jade ware of Liangzhu Culture had many more decorative patterns on the surface, making it more aesthetically pleasing than previous jade ware. The magnificent patterns, in particular, enhanced the artistic and visual effect of jade ware and inspired another brilliant chapter in the Chinese jade-ware history of the Neolithic Age.

Divine emblem with animal-faced god designs, Liangzhu Culture
The image expresses the concept of the god that was a combination of both human and beast.

At present, jade ware of Liangzhu Culture unearthed by archeological excavation numbers more than 10,000 pieces, and totals about 20,000 pieces worldwide if those held by overseas museums and private collectors are included. Such a large number was really unparalleled in the whole prehistoric jade culture, which not only shows the huge scale of jade processing and use, but also reflects the far-reaching influence of jade ware upon society at that time.

Craftsmanship during the Liangzhu Culture period was the peak of prehistoric jade-ware production and represented the ultimate level of jade working in South China. *Congs* (tubes with a square outer cross-section and circular inner cross-section) and *bi* (rings) made of bulk jade imposed very high requirements on jade extraction and cutting. Jade ware of Liangzhu Culture absorbed the techniques for jade ware of Lingjiatan Culture, boasting fairly mature carving techniques. Precise lines on jade surfaces, dense and intricately arranged, are as thin as hair. For

Jade *cong*, Liangzhu Culture.

Trifurcate jade ward, Liangzhu Culture
Made of yellow-white jade, it is divided into three, with a hole
pierced vertically in the middle. Its bottom is arc-shaped.

example, jade workers could engrave a complete divine symbol
composed of hundreds of lines within a very small area (3 cm ×
4 cm), demonstrating the superb jade-working techniques that
could not be replicated even with modern tools.

The people in the Liangzhu Culture period were extremely
engaged in jade-making techniques simply for complex and
mysterious pattern carving and further applications of such
patterns to communicate between humans and the gods. Nothing
else in the jade wares of Liangzhu Culture could be more
mysterious than the "god with an animal face" patterns that had
similar basic structures – the god, with an exaggerated face and
a magnificent, tall feather crown riding a mythical beast. The
patterns expressed the ancestors' wishes that humans could ride
horses to heaven and communicate with the gods, and suggested
the concept that humans were linked to heaven with jade ware,
thus serving as the best interpretation of the "jade for the gods"
theme. Abstract clan divine symbols could be found on all jade
wares like tubes, axes and gimlets and, as a result, Liangzhu

jade ware became the soul of Liangzhu Culture. The early people incorporated all their reverence to the gods and ancestors into the jade ware they made, and expressed their wishes to communicate with the gods through the "god with an animal face" patterns engraved on precious and magic jade materials, as they hoped that the gods to which they offered sacrifices could hear their inner voices and satisfy their needs.

A world-famous jade *cong*, unearthed from Pit No.12 at the Fanshan Liangzhu site located in Yuhang, Zhejiang Province in 1986, was crowned as "the King of Jade *cong*." It is 8.8 cm in height and 4.9 cm in diameter. The square jade *cong* is circular-shaped at the top and bottom, with a circular opening in the center. On its four sides are two groups of "god with an animal face" patterns, both the same: the upper part is the image of a god who has a broad trapezoid-shaped face, big eyes and noses and a wide mouth, and wears a crown with radial feather patterns and curling cloud (both the face and crown were carved with the bas-relief technique); and the lower part is an image of beast with two big eyes connected via a short line, a wide mouth with two pairs of buck teeth, squatting lower limbs and three-clawed feet. On the four corners of the jade *cong* were simplified "god with an animal face" patterns.

The shape mentioned above fully integrated the ideas the early people held about jade. Based on the theory of "Round Heaven and Square Earth" which prevailed in the Chinese prehistoric period, the *bi*, used to offer sacrifices to heaven, was round like "heaven," and the *cong*, used to offer sacrifices to earth, was square like the earth and had a band on each side that divided the surface into eight parts. This jade *cong* had slightly curved sides designed to symbolize earth, and two round ends to symbolize heaven, which showed that the people of the Liangzhu Culture period might already have thought of the space above the earth as heaven. The cylindrical opening running through the center of the jade *cong* was probably the means of connecting earth and heaven in the eyes of these early people. All these vividly described both the concept of earth and heaven, and existence as advocated by the people in Liangzhu Culture period.

The discovery of so many jade artifacts makes people today feel strongly about Liangzhu Culture and the amazing beauty of primitive religious art. The intricate designs and exquisite craftsmanship contained in this jade ware brings an entirely new meaning to prehistoric Chinese jade ware.

Jade Ware of the Longshan Culture

The Longshan Culture was a branch of the Neolithic Age Culture in the lower reaches of the Yellow River. Named after the Chengziya site in Longshan Town, Zhangqiu County, Shandong Province where it was first discovered, it existed around 3,500 to 4,000 years ago. The period saw a fundamental change in

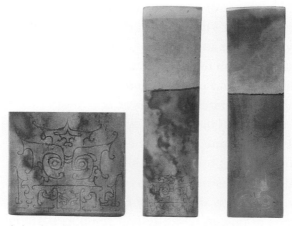

Jade adze with image of a beast's face, Longshan Culture.

ancient Chinese society and unprecedented progress in social productivity.

As the Longshan people mastered bronze-smelting techniques and applied them to jade processing, jade ware became finer and the techniques used were similar to those used in later periods. Embedding techniques emerged, evidenced by the jade axe with an embedded turquoise in its upper part unearthed in Shandong.

Central China was an area ruled by the legendary Yellow Emperor and Emperor Yan. The Longshan Culture period in Central China was a time of conflict between ancient

Jade pendant of "Eagle Clutching Human Heads," Longshan Culture.

kingdoms and the building of many fortifications. Most of the ancient cities were not just villages with ramparts; they were political, military, economic and religious centers as well. Jade ritual ware such as axes from the Longshan Culture carried both primitive religious beliefs and political concepts. Sacrificial tools evolved into symbols of hierarchy and power, and most of them have no signs of use though their shapes were almost the same as the stone tools of the same period. These jade ritual wares were separate from laboring tools and enjoyed a high status in terms of symbolism, suggesting the presence of a social class with privileges in production and military fields. Jade tools and weapons, as tokens of power, typically had complex patterns on their surfaces. This was the way people fully expressed their wishes on jade and suggested that jade ware had descended from the world of the gods to that of humans, although exclusively to royal and aristocratic families.

Jade ware of Longshan Culture, both in shape and style, generally showed signs of integration between the two great jade cultures in Northeast China and the areas south of the Yangtze River. Jade ware appeared in shapes never seen before, with jade tablets being the most common. The jade tablet, a ritual tool used by primitive people when offering sacrifices to heaven and ancestors, was considered to be capable of both entertaining the gods and ancestors and reassuring ordinary people, and hence thought to have a crucial role in connecting humans with heaven.

In 1963, cultural heritage workers acquired a jade tablet from two urban families in Rizhao, Shandong. The tablet is 18 cm tall, 4.9 cm in its widest part and 0.85 cm in its thickest part, with the top end, shaped like a flat blade with a slight arc resembling a stone adze. Made from a beautiful piece of jade, it has an incised abstract pattern depicting a god with extremely clear round eyes on its lower part. The pattern represents the wishes of the Longshan people that the omnipotent gods and ancestors would bring good luck to their clans and protect them from calamities.

The Palace Museum boasts a well-known piece called "Eagle Clutching Human Heads." The pendant, 9.1 cm long and 5.2 cm wide, was carved from a plate of grey jade. Its upper part is an eagle with round eyes, a hooked nose and a long crest, looking to one side and unfolding its wings, and in the claws of the eagle are two attractive human heads shown in profile. The jade pendant suggests that Longshan people offered sacrifices to the totem with human heads. According to ancient literature, the totem was used in such areas as Shandong during the prehistoric period. Sites of Longshan Culture in Hebei and Shaanxi provinces all saw discoveries of dismembered human bodies buried in abandoned wells and cellars. The pits might be those used to offer sacrifices with human heads, which were those of people from local tribes or captives in wars, but the true explanation remains unknown. Nevertheless, the phenomenon clearly suggests that the custom of offering sacrifices to ancestors and totems with human heads existed in the Longshan Culture period.

Prehistoric jade ware silently recorded a history without written languages, and pieces of jade ware engraved with the mysterious patterns of antiquity represent the spiritual beliefs of the primitive people. Jade ware in the Neolithic Age went beyond simple decorative, aesthetic purposes, and carried the sacred mission of connecting humans with gods and ancestors. Veiled in mystery, they became the medium helping humans communicate with the gods: thus, jade for the gods. This constituted the foundation of traditional Chinese culture and civilization.

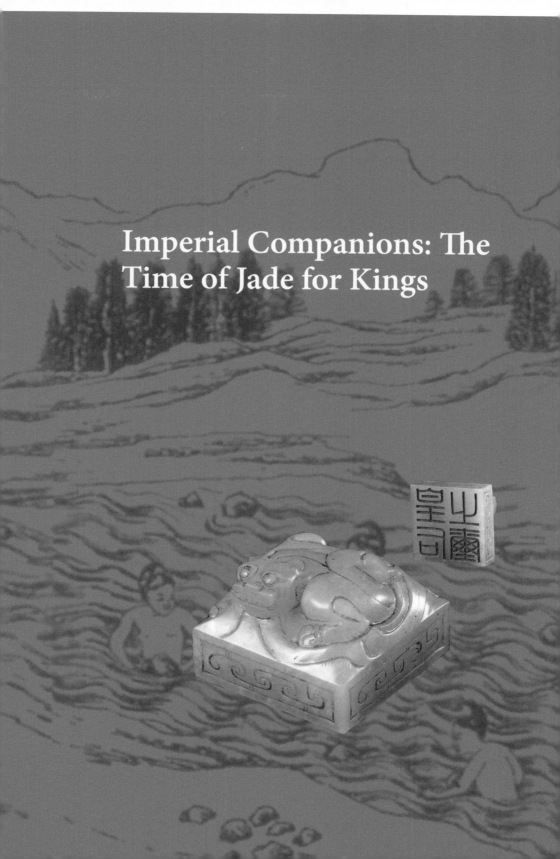

Imperial Companions: The Time of Jade for Kings

J ade ware descended from the world of the gods and stepped into human society from the Shang Dynasty to the periods of the Wei, Jin, Northern and Southern dynasties, but remained exclusive to royalty and nobility. Thus began the time of jade for kings, a period that saw the transition of China to a feudal society. Due to changes in society, Chinese jade ware developed continuously and Chinese jade culture was further enriched.

Jade Ware in the Shang Dynasty

The Shang Clan defeated the Xia Dynasty in the sixteenth century BC and founded the Shang Dynasty (1600–1046 BC). The Shang Dynasty frequently moved its capital and conquered neighboring clans in its early period, and its people learned advanced technologies and cultures wherever it went, further enriching the Shang Culture. Jades of diverse shapes and styles in the Shang Dynasty were the fruits of inheriting and carrying forward the essence of jade ware from earlier periods.

In the Shang Dynasty, jade and bronze wares developed in tandem and influenced each other, becoming one of the symbols of the highly developed civilization. The extraordinary achievements in jade ware were mainly attributed to the fact that the social division of labor between handicrafts and agriculture was completed shortly after the Shang Dynasty entered civilized society. The jade-making industry had grown as an independent handicraft sector boasting a large group of jade workers with outstanding skills and techniques. Inheritance and innovation of earlier jade-working craftsmanship by the people in the Shang Dynasty, as well as the great importance those wielding power attached to the jade industry, brought the jade ware of Shang Dynasty to a new peak.

Jade pendant with design of man kneeling, Shang Dynasty.

Ghost-god culture was at the core of the ideology of the Shang Dynasty. The Shang people had many sacrificial activities that combined jade ware with the gods, which was the most distinctive feature of jade use in the Shang Dynasty. Ancestral worship was thought to be capable of securing protection, and worship of the gods brought good luck and happiness. The round carved jade figurines with engraved clouds, thunder and beast face patterns were actually gods and ancestors in the eyes of the Shang people, while jade containers that were produced in the Shang Dynasty were ritual tools used to offer sacrifices to gods and ancestors.

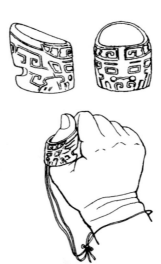

Jade *she*, a thumb ring, Shang Dynasty
Unearthed from the tomb of Fu Hao in
Anyang, Henan, it is mostly light green with
light brown parts. Hollow inside, it can be
worn on the thumb of an adult and has
beast images on its exterior. This *she* might
have been used by Fu Hao when she was
alive.

Instructions on use of jade *she*.

Among the jade figures unearthed from the Fu Hao Tomb in the Yin Ruins located in Anyang, Henan Province, a magnificently dressed jade man was the most eye-catching. The 7-cm-tall figurine was made of grey Hotan jade. Elegantly kneeling and resting his hands on his knees, he has a long braid coiling round his head, a long face, pointed chin, crescent-like thin eyebrows, a protruding nose and a closed mouth. Dressed in a cross-collar long robe with dense cloud patterns, he has a broad-handled instrument at his waist. Based on his splendid dress, noble manner and the mysterious instrument at his waist, it can be concluded that this might be the image of a noble slave owner who was the ancestor of merchants or the incarnation of a god. His kneeling posture reflects the common sitting position at that time. The elaborately made magnificent garment and exquisite craftsmanship make this figure a piece of extraordinary artwork.

The Shang Dynasty boasted diverse shapes of jade artifacts as a result of many innovations made by craftsmen. The most noteworthy is the *she*, which was designed to protect the fingers of an archer when drawing a bow string and shooting. This might be the predecessor of the thumb ring of the Qing Dynasty.

Jade crested man, Shang Dynasty
Made of reddish brown jade, a crested man squats; both sides of his body are basically symmetrical. This is the earliest flexible chain artwork known in China.

In the Shang Dynasty, use of bronze tools enhanced jade-making techniques significantly. Jade craftsmen at this time were also capable of skillfully combining such techniques as line carving, relief, carving in the round and fretwork, greatly increasing the range of artistic visual effects. Those beautiful and mysterious carved figurines and animal images of various sorts laid a foundation for the transition of ancient Chinese jade ware from simply decorated two-dimensional artwork to three-dimensional artwork with complex decoration.

The superb workmanship of jades in the Shang Dynasty was also embodied in its innovative techniques. Jades with linked rings first appeared in the Shang Dynasty. The crested human figure, unearthed from a tomb from the Shang Dynasty in Xin'gan of Jiangxi, has a chain composed of three rings behind his head, which is the earliest linked chain artwork ever discovered in China. Although the chain seems very simple, it was a great innovation in jade-working technology. Previously, people could only carve jade into items smaller than the starting material.

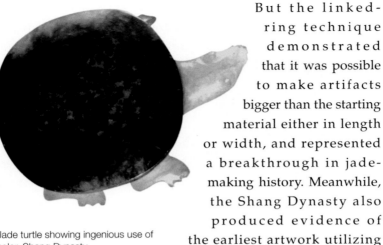

Jade turtle showing ingenious use of color, Shang Dynasty

But the linked-ring technique demonstrated that it was possible to make artifacts bigger than the starting material either in length or width, and represented a breakthrough in jade-making history. Meanwhile, the Shang Dynasty also produced evidence of the earliest artwork utilizing sophisticated techniques that used jade materials of different colors expressively. A jade turtle unearthed from the Yin Ruins in Henan Province shows superior craftsmanship integrating various colors. The turtle shell is black, while other parts are grey-white. The carved turtle, with its distinctive colors and vivid appearance, almost looks like the living creature. It is the earliest jade with such ingenious use of color yet discovered. One of the longest-living animals in nature, the turtle with its rounded shell and square-shaped body beneath reminded ancient people of the concept of "round heaven and square earth"; it was therefore considered as a spiritual being. In the Shang Dynasty, people even engraved the most sacred sacrificial words on turtle shells, so one can imagine that turtles enjoyed a very high status at that time. This piece of jade artwork, designed and made with the most advanced techniques available, implied the ancient worship of turtles.

The character "*Bao*" in oracle bone script in the Shang Dynasty resembled a house in which shellfish and jade were collected, suggesting that rulers of the Shang Dynasty regarded jade as treasure and wealth. This tradition of valuing jade as a precious

The jade figurine of Fu Hao

treasure continued and was fully embodied by a woman named Fu Hao in the Shang Dynasty. Fu Hao was one of sixty-four concubines of King Wu Ding of the Shang Dynasty. Her name appears in the oracle bone scripts from the Shang Dynasty no less than 170 times, as she was most loved by the king. During his fifty-nine-year reign, Wu Ding waged war on many places to conquer other clans, and Fu Hao often accompanied her husband to war. According inscriptions on oracle bones, Fu Hao once led a troop of 13,000 warriors in a battle when Emperor Wu Ding waged a war against the Qiang Clan, and even travelled a long distance to conquer the Tufang Kingdom in the northwestern areas. It is said that when Fu Hao died before Wu Ding, he was filled with such deep sorrow that he cried himself hoarse and often dreamed of meeting her. He ensured that Fu Hao was buried together with a great deal of jade ware. Although the tomb of Fu Hao was robbed and excavated before its discovery by archeologists, 750 pieces of jade ware were still unearthed in a formal excavation. The tomb of Fu Hao offers incontrovertible evidence regarding the importance of jade ware in the Shang Dynasty.

Jade ware in the Shang Dynasty not only perpetuated the concept of primitive worship, but also gradually personalized natural forces by incorporating human concepts. The primitive religious ideology symbolized in jade artifacts faded progressively and humanistic concepts became more significant. Hence, Chinese jade ware was ushered into a new era.

Jade Ware in the Western Zhou Dynasty

The Zhou people were part of an ancient clan in the northwestern part of China. The Western Zhou Dynasty (1046–771 BC) was the period that witnessed the peak of the Chinese ritual system, praised as exemplary by Confucius (551–479 BC) whose philosophy, which influenced China for thousands of years, was based on such a ritual theory. As vast amounts of archeological material and literature prove, the Western Zhou Dynasty was a period when jade use in ancient China developed and jade was first endowed with moral connotations. This had a far-reaching influence upon later generations.

The use of jade with different qualities and colors was strictly established in the Western Zhou Dynasty, resulting in the presence of a colorful jade world including white, grey, black and green artifacts. White jade was preferred in the Western Zhou Dynasty, and precious Hotan jade was particularly favored. In addition, there were many other popular materials like agate, crystal and turquoise. Rulers of the Western Zhou Dynasty

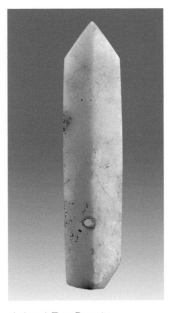

Jade *gui*, Zhou Dynasty

typically adopted expensive jade ware such as white Hotan jade; common jade ware suggesting lower social status were usually made of other types of jade. The diversity of jade in the Western Zhou Dynasty was not only the result of feudal hierarchy, but also reflected the advanced level of the jade-working industry at that time.

The ritual system was important in Chinese slave societies, particularly in the Western Zhou Dynasty. In fact, the rites from remote periods were sacrificial ceremonies of clan members, while the Zhou people later developed them into a complete patriarchal system. Jade ware at this time naturally became tools serving the hierarchical system advocated by the rulers, and the "six *ruis*" (six ritual instruments), "six *qis*" (six sacrificial instruments) and group pendants were evidence of this societal development.

The "six *ruis*" referred to six kinds of jade artifact. The "*ruis*" here were ranks of nobility that the imperial court awarded to senior officials. King, duke, marquis, count, viscount and baron

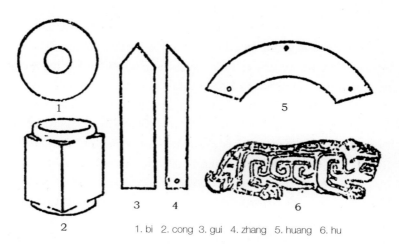

1. bi 2. cong 3. gui 4. zhang 5. huang 6. hu

The six sacrificial jade instruments recorded in *The Rites of Zhou*

were the six ranks of nobility, who would respectively hold jade *"gui"* and *"bi."* According to *The Rites of Zhou*: "The six *ruis* made of jade symbolize different ranks. Kings shall hold *zhen gui*, dukes hold *huan gui*, marquises hold *xin gui*, counts hold *gong gui*, viscounts hold *gu bi* and barons hold *pu bi*."

The "six *qis*" were also recorded in *The Rites of Zhou*: "The six *qis* made of jade are used as sacrificial instruments. The blue *bi* is used to offer sacrifices to heaven, the yellow *cong* for earth, the black *gui* for the eastern world, the red *zhang* for the southern world, the white *hu* for the western world and the black *huang* for the northern world." The above instruments in six different colors were needed in sacrificial ceremonies at that time, and reflected the development of ritual jade as instruments to offer sacrifices to natural gods. Jade artifacts had become the best tools to display ritual relationships through outer forms.

Among all the ritual jade ware in the Western Zhou Dynasty, the most distinctive is the group pendant, a special ornament with ritual attributes. Dominated by jade *huang*, an arc-shaped ornament, it consisted of different parts that were connected with each other based on certain rules. According to the fact that most of the jade group pendants from the Western Zhou Dynasty appeared in the tombs of kings and their wives and sons, it can be concluded there was a rigid system for how large jade group pendants were used. The excavated materials also show that the jade group pendants have two features: (i) The numbers of *huang* in various group pendants are different, perhaps identifying the user's social status; (ii) pieces of jade are usually separated by agate, stone, glass and turquoise beads, which is in line with the ritual system stipulated in *The Rites of Zhou* that ministers of kings could not use pure jade. The jade group pendants may have only been used by rulers of kingdoms such as dukes, marquises and their wives, or aristocrats with equivalent titles.

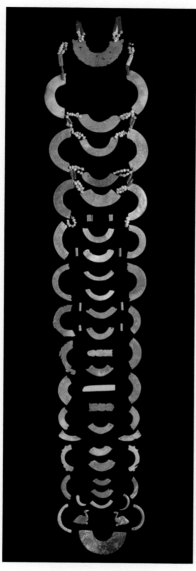

Jade group pendant, Western Zhou Dynasty
Unearthed from Pit No. 63 of the tomb of a Marquis of the State of Jin in Quwo County, Shanxi Province, the pendant consists of 204 pieces of jade ornaments including jade *huang*, jade *heng*, jade tubes, turquoise beads and agate tubes.

A jade group pendant unearthed from the tomb of Jinhou in Quwo County of Shanxi Province consists of 204 pieces of jade including forty-five *huangs* that are arranged in three lines and have double dragon patterns. On the upper part of the pendant are two lively geese raising their heads and necks to the sky. This huge jade group pendant is magnificent enough to show the noble status of the tomb occupant.

As the Zhou people matched heaven with virtue, jade ware was abstractly considered to be the carrier of morality and thus played a role in establishing and consolidating ethical relationships in religious and legal hierarchical systems. The "six *ruis*," "six *qis*" and jade group pendants that had distinctive hierarchical meanings are physical proof of this system. The development of jade culture in the Western Zhou Dynasty led to the later inclusion of jade ware in the moral scope and formation of the concept of "a gentleman compares virtues to a gem."

Another jade artifact with a unique style appeared in the Western Zhou Dynasty.

Combining both human and dragon bodies, the piece inspires the imagination and embodies the special relationship between the Zhou people and the dragon. Prehistoric humans believed all creatures had spirits, hence the development of primitive nature worship and the dragon image. With social progress as well as the gradual establishment of humans' position in nature and the development of their consciousness of power, the dragon, a representative of those adored by humans, was endowed with human features and further personified. A "person-dragon" jade ornament, unearthed from the tomb of Jinhou, was placed on the abdomen of the tomb occupant when found. Made of brown jade, it is 2.9 cm tall and 4.5 cm long. This ornament is a combination of a crested man and a dragon body. The crested man is in front of the dragon, with finely chiseled facial features and his lower part connected with the dragon's body. The dragon looks behind and its tail curls slightly up. This ornament, with its unique shape

A "person-dragon" jade ornament, Western Zhou Dynasty
A combination of crested man and dragon, the brown jade has the same design on both sides. Carved with fretwork technique, the images consist of double hook and single carved lines.

and mysterious meaning, embodies the special relationship between humans and dragons in the eyes of the Zhou people. So, jade art integrating humans and dragons truly describes the need of the Zhou people to personalize natural forces. In a word, no signs of primitive worship could be found in the jade ware of the Western Zhou Dynasty; instead, jade ware as combinations of both forms and spirits took shape, carrying the inner feelings and wishes of human beings.

Jade ware in the Western Zhou Dynasty connected the past and later periods, boasting many innovations in categories, shapes and patterns. They displayed new styles of jade culture, in particular the trend of linking jade ware with humans, and became the foundation of jade ware in the Spring and Autumn Period and Warring States Period.

Jade Ware in the Spring and Autumn Period

The Spring and Autumn Period (770–476 BC) and Warring States Period (475–221 BC) were times when ancient Chinese society underwent significant changes. Vassals of all states contended for hegemony during this period of great social turbulence and disruption. But the fractured political situation, instead of curbing economic and cultural progress, greatly boosted exchanges in these two areas. It was the same with jade culture at this time.

With the collapse of the hierarchical system of the Western Zhou Dynasty, the Spring and Autumn Period saw great changes in people's ideology and aesthetic concepts. Meanwhile, social development and scientific progress enlightened the people

Jade *bi*, Spring and Autumn Period
Made of dark and light green jade, the round *bi* has white
spots caused by corrosion. It has a total of 124 dragon
designs on both sides, with two circles featuring smooth and
thin lines carved on both the outer and inner rims.

and helped them to move beyond primitive god worship. Thus, jade ware creation, rather than being a matter of awe towards ghosts and gods, took a path of consciously manifesting human personalities. The purpose of aesthetic consciousness also gradually shifted from entertaining the gods in early periods to entertaining humans. To cater to the political and aesthetic needs of the aristocracy and wealthy merchants who had become the dominant forces in society, jade was adopted to embody contemporary trends of thought. This made jade culture flourish further, incorporating the concept of "comparing virtues to a gem" from the Western Zhou Dynasty, and finally helped form the theoretic system of the Chinese jade known as "a gentleman comparing virtues to a gem."

The philosopher Confucius, the founder of Confucianism, elaborated fully on the thought of "a gentleman comparing virtues to a gem." In Confucius's view, jade's soft sheen represented benevolence. Jade is hard to break and would not hurt skin even when broken, which could be compared to justice. Jade pendants were tidy and orderly, which represented courtesy. Jade produces a pleasing sound when struck, which symbolizes joy. Its flaws and pure parts would never mix, which represented royalty. Everyone loved and cherished jade, which could be compared to morals and other such good values. *The Book of Rites*, incorporating the words of Confucius, closely links the natural attributes of jade to Confucian morals and summarizes eleven virtues: benevolence, wisdom, justice, courtesy, joy, royalty, faith, heaven, earth, morals and ethics. These helped establish the theoretical foundation of the Confucian jade system with benevolence as its core, and became the criteria for gentlemen in conducting themselves in society with self-discipline, and the moral codes for scholar officials. Jade was thus extolled for its great virtues.

The personalization of jade ware highlighted the concept that jade, in nature, embodied the noble spiritual world and self-discipline of humans more than their physical beauty. As society advanced and civilized, jade ware was combined with more practical utility and social meanings. Not every member of society had the privilege of using jade, as it was still exclusive to royal families and nobles. Moreover, the convention that "a gentleman in the ancient times must wear a jade pendant" gradually appeared. Carrying group pendants also had the following functions: first, gentlemen walked in an elegant manner. Jade pendants in groups could not produce an orderly sound unless the wearer walked at a moderate and rhythmic pace. Years later, gentlemen would develop a regular and elegant style of walking under the constraint of jade pendants. Second, gentlemen behaved with decorum. The group pendants would tell others where the wearer went as they tinkled as he walked. Hence, the convention of "a gentleman shall always carry a jade pendant" appeared as part of a society with rigid ritual systems.

The custom of wearing jade pendants was needed not only to cultivate the minds of gentlemen, but also played a role in reinforcing the hierarchical nature of society. This was the same in the Spring and Autumn Period when the ritual system almost collapsed. An example of transgression of customary jade use that happened in the State of Lu was recorded in the *Zuo Zhuan* (*Zuo's Commentary on the Spring and Autumn Annals*): In the fifth year of the reign of Lu Dinggong (505 BC), Ji Pingzi, who had controlled state power for over thirty years, died. His retainer Yang Hu attempted to bury the *yufan*, a jade pendant that could

Image of Confucius, founder of Confucianism.

only be carried by the King of Lu, in Ji Pingzi's tomb. However, Ji's other retainer did not agree to the practice and required that they "change both his status and jade pendant." That is to say, although Ji Pingzi had taken the place of the King in exercising state power and had worn a *yufan* to offer sacrifices in the ancestral temple in Lu Zhaogong's (Lu Dinggong's predecessor as King) absence, Ji Pingzi had to revert to his status as a minister and wear the jade pendant that was suitable for a minister because Lu Dinggong had assumed the throne. Although Ji

Pingzi was a figure that once exercised supreme power in the State of Lu, and had even sent Lu Zhaogong into exile, such a powerful political figure was still marginalized in the jade-use system, revealing the rigid social hierarchy.

Wearing jade pendants was associated with the spiritual world, words, conduct, and moral cultivation. As a way of conveying ambition through physical materials, jade was used to show the character, sentiments, qualities, and grace of the owner. Jade ware at this time was strictly regulated by the new rites, ethics, and moral codes. Shapes, weights, sizes, colors or patterns symbolized the ethical and social concepts of the time. Every piece of jade ware, therefore, had certain political, ethical and religious meanings.

During the Spring and Autumn Period, jade was compared to the virtues of gentlemen, equating beautiful jade with great human virtues. An event was recorded in the Gongye Chang chapter of *The Analects of Confucius*, where Zi Gong asked his teacher Confucius, "How do you think of me?" Confucius

Tiger-shaped jade ornament, Spring and Autumn Period
Made of slate-grey jade, this piece is flat. The tiger, bowing its head, with its back hunched, its limbs bent and curling its tail, seems to be jumping and displays a kind of inner spiritual power.

Jade sword ornament, Spring and Autumn Period
Aristocrats in the Spring and Autumn Period not only carried jade themselves, but also attached jade to their swords. This sword ornament, made of semi-transparent grey jade, boasts a soft sheen and superb texture, and is one of the finest among the jade sword ornaments from this period.

replied, "You're like a *hulian*." The *hulian* mentioned here was a ritual utensil used to hold sacrificial offerings. Embedded with expensive, beautiful jade ornaments, *hulian* was the most precious of all utensils and was thus compared to a talented person capable of holding the political power of a nation. In Confucius's eyes, Zi Gong was such a man.

As for the jades in the Spring and Autumn Period, their profound ethical value was obviously greater than aesthetic and artistic values. Gentlemen who carried jade pendants regarded them as more than just beautiful ornaments; they aimed to show their virtues and jade-like noble qualities. In addition, exquisite jade ornaments also made royalty and nobility look wealthier.

The two sides of jade, the outer ornaments and their token of inner virtues, complemented and integrated with each other, bringing Chinese jade culture to another new historical peak and laying a sound foundation for the development of jade ware in the Warring States Period.

Jade Ware in the Warring States Period

The Warring States Period was a dramatic time in Chinese history, witnessing ceaseless wars among all states. The battles promoted cultural progress to a certain extent and exerted a far-reaching influence upon the development of jade ware in the Warring States Period.

Wood figurine in a robe of two colors, Warring States Period
This statue was unearthed from the tomb of the State of Chu in Wuchang, Jiangling, Hubei. On both sides of the figurine's chest hangs a group of jade ornaments, which confirms the ancient Chinese saying, "a gentleman shall always carry a jade pendant."

During this period, people had better knowledge of jade materials and could distinguish them from common stones more precisely, as told in the legend of the *He Shi Bi*. This recounts how a jade craftsman in the State of Chu, Bian He, once discovered piece of jade that, though it looked like a stone, was judged by him as precious jade based on his knowledge and experience. He presented the piece of jade to King Li of Chu who, however, did not believe it was jade and ordered that the right foot of Bian He be cut off, saying the man had cheated him. After the king died, Bian He presented the jade to King Wu of Chu who also did not believe it was jade and cut off Bian He's left foot. It was not until King Wen of Chu took the throne that the jade was discovered to be the very best quality jade and thus named as *He Shi Bi*. The story shows that jade craftsmen in the Warring States Period were able to go beyond the outer appearance of jade and see its nature, and also reflects how the people at that time loved and cherished jade.

The Warring States Period saw a greater number of jade artifacts made of Hotan jade and significant progress was made in jade-carving techniques and decoration. It is most noteworthy that jade craftsmen in the Warring States Period could make full use of jade materials to carve exquisite artwork. A dragon-phoenix-shaped jade ornament composed of sixteen parts was unearthed from the tomb of Marquis Yi of Zeng in Hubei Province in 1978. Made of white Hotan jade, it is 48 cm long and 8.3 cm wide. With several carved dragons and phoenixes that are connected with rings and a pin, the whole constitutes a long dragon-shaped ornament, and each part moves flexibly. This artifact was so ingeniously designed and exquisitely made that it amazed jade connoisseurs. The jade craftsmen during this time made large jade ornaments from smaller pieces, separately carving pieces that were then connected, which not only saved both labor and jade

Dragon and phoenix-shaped pendants made of sixteen pieces of jade, Warring States Period

This jade pendant consists of sixteen parts that are carved into dragon, phoenix, *bi*, or ring shapes. Various parts are connected by three rings and a pin, and each part moves flexibly.

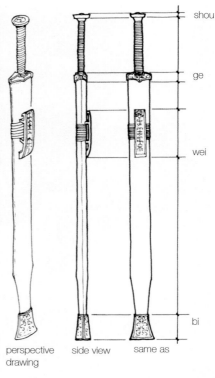

shou

ge

wei

bi

perspective
drawing

side view

same as

Jade sword ornament, Warring States Period
Jade sword ornaments prevailed in the Spring and
Autumn Period as well as the Western and Eastern
Han dynasties. This set of jade sword ornaments are
all white, similar in color to chicken bone.

Sketch of jade swords

materials, but also made the jade ornament appear symmetrical
and beautiful. This splendid multi-part jade ornament was placed
beside the jaw of the Marquis Yi of Zeng when it was found and
was probably one of his most cherished personal belongings.

Jade ware in the Warring States Period had more categories
than ever before. To cater for the decorative needs of the nobles,
jade ornaments such as *huangs*, group ornaments, dragon-
phoenixes, coiling dragon patterns and dancing figure patterns

Dragon-shaped jade ornaments, Warring States Period
This pair of jade ornaments, unearthed from the tomb of Marquis Yi of Zeng, are
made of grey jade with brown spots. The dragons have thin, twisting bodies, and are
decorated with cloud patterns mixed with grain-like patterns.

were in mass production, and utilitarian jade items, such as
belt hooks and sword fittings became parts of nobles' belts and
swords.

Dragon-shaped jade ware in the Warring States Period was
diversified. The dragons had sharp eyes and teeth, showing
the ferocious side of the mythical animal; they puffed their
chests out and raised their tails high, looking lively, aggressive
and vigorous. The S-shaped twisting dragon-like ornaments,
lively and humorous, came in a large variety in styles. A pair of
dragon-like jade ornaments excavated from the tomb of Marquis
Yi of Zeng manifests the aforementioned dynamic vigor. The
ornaments, made of grey jade, are 11.5 cm high, 8 cm wide and 0.6
cm thick. With a long, thin twisting body, the dragon is S-shaped

and covered with beautiful cloud and grain patterns. These are the best interpretations of the diverse culture in the Warring States Period, resulting from a situation in which all vassals contended for hegemony, leading to a brilliant chapter in Chinese jade culture.

Jade ware became a token of wealth during the Warring States Period. There were no kings or nobles who did not regard jade as a precious treasure. Jade ware not only represented individual wealth, but was also an integral part of national wealth. As a result of the frequent diplomatic activities that accompanied the continuous wars among states, jade artifacts were received as precious gifts in the exercise of diplomacy. Jade ware was loved and pursued by rulers of all states to an extent never seen before, as was shown in the case of "Returning the Jade Intact to the State of Zhao," a wonderful story that described the State of Qin and the State of Zhao in the Warring States Period vying to win a piece of jade *bi*.

This story was also related to *He Shi Bi*. In the late Warring States Period, King Huiwang of the State of Zhao acquired the *He Shi Bi*, an exquisite piece of jade from the State of Chu. Upon hearing the news, King Zhaowang of the State of Qin immediately sent a letter to King Huiwang of the State of Zhao, saying he was willing to exchange the *He Shi Bi* for fifteen of his cities. King Huiwang of the State of Zhao dispatched Lin Xiangru to the State of Qin together with the *He Shi Bi*. When Lin Xiangru presented the *He Shi Bi* to King Zhaowang of the State of Qin, he was most joyful and passed the jade *bi* to others for appreciation, but did not mention fulfillment of his bargain of exchanging it for cities. Lin Xiangru, noticing that the King of the State of Qin did not intend to honor his commitment, devised a stratagem and calmly walked up to the King of Qin, saying: "The *He Shi Bi* has a little flaw. Let me show it to you." The King of Qin did not know the truth and returned the jade *bi* to Lin who,

Returning the jade intact to the State of Zhao

upon receiving the jade, suddenly retreated to the stone column. "King Huiwang had engaged in five fast days for the jade's trip to the State of Qin and then sent me here, which shows how serious King Huiwang is! But when you get the jade, you treat it too lightly, casually showing it to others. Since you do not have the intention to exchange the fifteen cities, I will have my head hit against the wall along with the jade if you force me to give it to you," Lin scolded angrily, and held the *He Shi Bi* towards the column, ready to break it. The King of Qin loved the jade so much that he hurriedly apologized to Lin. As he asked the King of Qin to quickly choose another auspicious day for the jade exchange, Lin sent another person to secretly return the *He Shi Bi* to the State of Zhao. When the King of Qin found out what happened, he could do nothing and had to let Lin go back to the State of Zhao.

In ancient China a hero would protect valuable jade even at the cost of their own life. In the story "Returning the Jade Intact to the State of Zhao," a jade *bi* is worth fifteen cities, reflecting the ancient saying that "Gold is expensive, but jade is invaluable."

Later, the *He Shi Bi* belonged to the State of Qin. The Emperor Qinshihuang had it made into the imperial jade seal with the inscription of *"Shou ming yu tian, ji shou yong chang"* ("Becoming the emperor by the grace of the gods, the imperial power will be long-lasting and flourish") written by Prime Minister Li Si. It became the first jade imperial seal owned by Chinese emperors and symbolized supreme imperial power. Meanwhile, a decree was issued that all seals used in royal families should be made of jade and called *xi*, and all private seals, no matter what materials they were made of, should be called *yin* or *zhang*. Although jade imperial seals were made by all dynasties from the Qin Dynasty, all rulers hoped to get the jade seal of Emperor Qinshihuang as they believed only this could make the world believe they were true emperors by the grace of the gods. The jade imperial seal was fought over in bloody wars for centuries and then disappeared after it had passed into the hands of Emperor Modi, the last emperor of the later Tang Dynasty, in the tenth century.

Jade Ware in the Han Dynasty

The Han Dynasty (206 BC–AD 220) could be divided into three phases: the Western Han Dynasty, Xinmang Period and the Eastern Han Dynasty. The establishment and development of the unified multi-ethnic feudal country in the Western Han Dynasty brought ancient China into a golden era. After more than 400 years of development achieved in the Western and Eastern Han Dynasties, Chinese culture began to take shape.

While inheriting the traditional features of the Warring States Period, especially the fresh, graceful and romantic styles of those in previous dynasties, jade ware in the Han Dynasty developed a bold and unconstrained artistic style typical of the dynasty and thus brought ancient Chinese jade ware to another peak.

In Chinese jade history, the Han Dynasty saw a new epoch in the use of white jade, particularly the white Hotan jade and the "sheep-fat" white jade, both in quantity and in quality. This can be attributed to two phenomena: the Han empire opened a route to the western regions, which made the traffic between the eastern and western regions operate more smoothly and the Hotan jade from Xinjiang was continuously transported into Central China; and, as a result of the prevailing doctrine of "Yin-Yang" and the "Five Elements," people regarded white as an auspicious color and placed the concept of "advocating white" on a par with Confucianism, which enhanced the cultural meaning of color in jade ware and endowed it with moral implications.

Jade ware in the Han Dynasty, through practical and exaggerated means of creation, combined the romantic life of the immortals in heaven with the practical world and a strong sense of reality. Besides the traditional immortal spirits like the dragon and phoenix, which were believed to be capable of warding off evil spirits and bringing good luck, the "evil-averting" beast, dragon-tiger and divine horse also became artistic images that were popular, said to be able to fly in space, communicate with the immortals and carry humans into the sky. Jade ware in the Han Dynasty appeared unconstrained and romantic. A jade running horse from the Western Han Dynasty, unearthed from Shaanxi Province, has four exaggerated limbs and two wings, raising its head high, it appears to fly in the cloudy sky. On its back sits a serious, elite immortal. The artwork appears dynamic

Dancing figure-shaped jade ornaments, Western Han Dynasty
These two jade figurines have the same images, clothes and dancing postures. With long eyes, thin eyebrows, prominent noses, small mouths and elliptical faces, they are presenting "the raising sleeves and curved waist" dance that was popular in the Qin and Han Dynasties.

and is full of intensity, showing how the ancient people longed for a fantasy world and portrayed the great and noble spirits of the time.

The dragon-tiger patterns carved on swords are more appealing. The dragon-tigers, strong and vigorous, have diverse shapes: they either jump into the clouds with bodies coiled and heads raised or play joyfully in the sky. Their strong, plump bodies, high spirits and harmonious and lively appearances, broke with the traditional style manifested in jade artifacts of early periods and became the brilliant artistic representatives in jade ware of the Han Dynasty.

Jade carving art in the Han Dynasty abandoned the previous flat plate shapes and was concentrated more on high relief and

Jade immortal riding a horse, Western Han Dynasty

The running horse steps on a ball-like object with its front hoof. On the back of the horse is a crested man who is holding the horse's neck with one hand and holding a *reishi* in the other. The cloud patterns carved on the pedestal implies the horse is running in the sky.

Eight Carving Lines of the Han Dynasty: The style typical of the Han Dynasty, meant that the carvings could be finished after only "eight carving lines" and reflected the style of carvings that were characterized by simplicity and conciseness. However, the so-called "Eight Carving Lines of the Han Dynasty" did not really mean the eight carving lines could finish a piece of jade work, but demonstrated the simple and skilled carving techniques that could make jade artwork vivid and lively. Jade pigs held in hands were one of the representative works of the Eight Carving Lines of the Han Dynasty.

round carving. The jade cicadas and pigs of the Han Dynasty fully display the vitality of the animals through plain forms and the simple carving techniques known as the "Eight Carving Lines of the Han Dynasty," were one of the most distinctive expressive means adopted in ancient Chinese carving. As for the shapes of the jade ware, jade artisans in the Han Dynasty highlighted outlines and abandoned details to make the general effect better and fully displayed the spirits of the objects, which reflected real life and the good wishes of the ancient people.

One imperial seal in the Han Dynasty is most noteworthy among all the ritual jade of the period. A primary school student picked up an imperial seal from the Han Dynasty in a field ditch near the mountain ranges located in Hanjiawan, Xianyang of Shaanxi in 1968, and handed it to the State. When confirmed by the cultural heritage authority as the "seal of the Empress" in the Han Dynasty, it immediately received wide attention. The seal is 2 cm high, 2.8 cm long and weighs 33g. Made of Hotan jade from Xinjiang, it is square-shaped and has dragon-tiger patterns, with four characters *"Huang hou zhi xi"* (the seal of the Empress) carved on the bottom. Jade was first made into seals in the Warring States Period, and imperial seals of the Qin and Han dynasties had long been considered lost, so when the "seal

Seal of the empress, Western Han Dynasty

of the Empress" was discovered, it quickly became a rare treasure and gave the world an opportunity to appreciate the splendor of imperial seals over 2,000 years old.

Funeral jade in particular prevailed in the Han Dynasty. As a nation of rites and ceremonies, the Chinese had long practiced the tradition of extravagant funerals and regarded it as a part of the ritual system. As a result, a full set of jade ware especially designed to protect bodies from decaying appeared. Royal and noble families in the Han Dynasty used jade clothes to wrap bodies. Each set of jade clothing appeared the same size as the real body and could be divided into six parts, including the head cover, upper body cover, sleeves, gloves, trousers and shoes, all made of small rectangular jade plaques and stitched together with gold, silver and copper threads. The different materials represented the social status of the deceased. According to *The Book of the Later Han*, emperors used jade clothes with gold carved patterns, while dukes, marquises, court ladies and princesses used those with silver carved patterns, and great court ladies and the princesses royal used those with copper carved patterns. There were strict provisions for the use of jade clothes that could

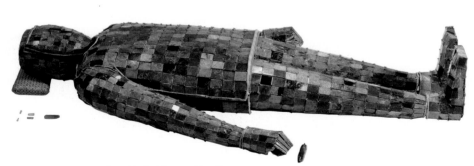

Jade clothes sewn with gold silk, Western Han Dynasty
Unearthed from a Han Dynasty tomb in the Xishan Mountain, Mangshan Town, Yongsheng city, Henan Province, it is presently in the Henan Museum collection. The whole set of jade clothes consists of 2,008 plaques of jade, which were connected with silk.

not go beyond the Han Dynasty, particularly the Western Han Dynasty. Rulers invested heavily in making jade clothes in the hope of protecting their bodies from decay by resorting to the magic power of jade and thus helping their souls ascend into heaven. However, the jade ware and other gold and silver jewelry buried along with the tomb occupants attracted numerous tomb raiders. During the reign of Emperor Wendi of the State of Wei (187–226), Cao Pi, seeing that all tombs of the Han Dynasties were robbed, forbade extravagant funerals. This brought an end to the use of jade clothes and extravagant funerals that prevailed in the Han Dynasty.

Taoism and metaphysics were advocated during the Han Dynasty. Royal princes and nobles prayed for immortal lives and longed to go to heaven. Ordinary people also yearned towards the land that was totally different from the mundane world. Affected by such ideas, concepts contained in jade ware, such as ancestor worship, rites, codes and morals dating from the Shang and Zhou dynasties were changed, and jade ware became a bridge going beyond life and death, connecting immortals with real people, as well as a carrier of people's immortal dreams that would last for thousands of years. The idea of immortal life in the Han Dynasty was displayed in a jade table screen that described a fairytale. The table screen is made of four plates carved with fretwork techniques. The four jade plates are placed on the brackets on both sides and the upper and lower layers in the middle, with the tenons of the two pieces in the middle inserted into the slots in both brackets. The Eastern King and Western Queen were the gods in the east and west respectively in the myths of antiquity. In the very center of the upper part of the jade screen is the image of the legendary Eastern King who is sitting on a high throne beside the table and is accompanied by fairies and phoenixes. In the center of the lower part of the screen is the Western Queen who is also sitting on a high throne beside

Jade vessel, Han Dynasty
The cylindrical vessel was made of corroded pink white jade, with patterns of dragon-tiger, dragon, bear, and immortals on clouds carved on its outer surface and three bear legs under its flat bottom. It reflects ideas about the existence of gods during the Han Dynasty.

the table, accompanied by fairies and divine beasts. The screen is flawless in carving technique and looks like a line-drawing. It naturally incorporates figures, scenes, and animals. The artwork is the only of its kind discovered so far and reflects the ideology of people who longed for harmonious, romantic and happy lives.

Jade ware in the Han Dynasty startled the world with its bold, unconstrained, fresh, unique style, and those pieces made with round carving, high relief and fretwork techniques became the mainstream of jade ware in the Han Dynasty. These jade items also abandoned religious and ritual meanings and pursued a different artistic value. This trend dominated the development of ancient Chinese jade ware in the following 2,000 years.

Jade Ware in the Wei, Jin, Northern and Southern Dynasties

The period of Wei, Jin, Southern and Northern dynasties included the Three Kingdoms Period (220–280), the Western Jin Dynasty (265–317), the Eastern Jin Dynasty (317–420), and the Southern and Northern dynasties (420–589). Social and political developments in this period curbed the development of jade ware. Jade wares at this time were just a continuation of the fashions of the Han Dynasty, with a dramatic decrease in numbers, less innovation, and relatively smaller number of Hotan jade artwork. This suggests that jade ware became less popular during this time, marking the end of the time of jade for kings.

Amber exotic beast, the Southern Dynasties

Made of brown amber and carved in the round, this beast sits on its heels with its front paws crossed in front of its chest with cicada patterns on its back.

The main reasons for this situation are: first, the court explicitly banned extravagant funerals, which was the direct reason for the decreased demand for funerary jade; second, numerous wars affected the transportation of jade materials, and this shook the core industry of jade-ware making; third, metaphysics prevailed in the Wei and Jin dynasties, and nobles and scholar officials who advocated a free life tried to get rid of traditional rites, which resulted in less ritual jade making; fourth, Buddhist culture and associated artwork suddenly gained popularity, hence the construction of many stone Buddhist carvings such as the Yungang and Longmen Grottes. Numerous jade workers were attracted into this new field of the craft, affecting jade-ware making; fifth, the sudden rise of porcelain as well as gold and silver ware also had a certain impact on the development of jade ware; finally, a dramatic decrease in the amount of jade ware was associated with the trend of "eating jade." There was a belief that consuming jade could make one immortal at this time;

Jade goat, Wei and Jin Dynasties
This animal was made of grey-white jade with yellow spots on its surface. The goat slightly raises its head, with both eyes open wide and looking straight ahead; its long horns curl behind its ears.

this was the peak of superstition towards jade since the Han Dynasty. Influenced by this idea of immortality and the alchemy of necromancers, much jade ware from previous dynasties was powdered and destroyed.

However, jade ware in this period did have unique features. These included pieces that were carvings of legendary beasts and ghosts. The beasts, usually with distorted appearances, were combinations of humans and animals with wings, which might be a metaphor for the turbulence in society.

The period of Wei, Jin, and Southern and Northern dynasties was not a great time for Chinese jade ware, especially when compared to that of the Han and Tang dynasties. It was a transitional period that witnessed the withdrawal of ritual and funerary jade from the historical stage and the beginning of jade for simple decoration and appreciation. Afterwards, Chinese jade was secularized from the political and hierarchical world, which marked a new age, ushering in the time of jade for the people.

Enter Civil Society: The Time of Jade for the People

With the social changes that occurred between the Sui and Tang dynasties and the Qing Dynasty, jade ware gradually departed from the exclusive domain of royalty and nobility to include the public at large – or at least the wealthy. Chinese jade ware thus entered a new era. Royal families and nobles remained the largest consumer group of jade ware, but the difference lay in changes in the jade-use system and cultural meanings. With the arrival of jade for the people, decorative subjects for jade ware were much richer than those in previous dynasties and expressed with more realistic methods. Auspicious patterns with

This is a gold-rimmed jade *die xie* belt embedded with pearls from the Tang Dynasty. It boasts lavish decoration and superb craftsmanship.

distinctive national features were very popular among the people, boasting rich content and implications. Everything from flowers, grass, fish and insects, to birds and beasts were endowed with different symbolic meanings and used to symbolize good fortune and elegant temperaments. Much of the artwork had patterns with auspicious implications, which reflected the aesthetic consciousness of the public and the people's hopes for a better life. Jade ware from the Sui and Tang dynasties, despite becoming daily decorative objects, remained a physical carrier of people's spirits and desires. Chinese jade culture in this period entered a new chapter, and remains charming to this day.

Jade Ware in the Tang Dynasty

Li Yuan (r. 618–626), Emperor Gaozu, founded the Tang Dynasty (618–907) in 618. The rule of the Tang Dynasty for nearly 300 years represented the apogee of Chinese feudal society. Stable politics, a flourishing economy, and frequent diplomatic agreements created the splendid culture of the Tang Dynasty and attracted worldwide attention. There were innovations in the quality, categories, and style of jade ware. The superb carving techniques and unique shaping showed that ancient Chinese jade ware regained its splendor. Jade ware in the Tang Dynasty not only reflected the technique and art inherited from previous generations. It also provided inspiration for later jade ware production, giving it an important place in the history of Chinese jade.

The Tang Dynasty enjoyed a developed economy and culture as well as a prosperous handicraft industry. Jade continued to play a crucial role in the material culture represented by jade ware, pottery, bronze mirrors and gold and silver ware. Monarchs and aristocrats all regarded jades as luxurious ornaments, while jade ware at this time was not simply exclusive to their circles, but started its journey to the public.

Jade ware in the Tang Dynasty would not have been so brilliant without the contributions of the jade-working center of the city of Yangzhou. Since Emperor Suiyang (reigned 604–618) built the Grand Canal, the city had been affluent and prosperous, with its handicrafts including metal smelting, architecture, ship building, gold and silver ware, lacquer, wood ware and bronze mirrors. Among these crafts, jade working gradually flourished. Yangzhou was first established as a jade-working center during the Tang Dynasty, and this laid a solid foundation for art and craft in the Ming and Qing dynasties.

Grand Beijing-Hangzhou Canal: The 1,700-km-long canal starts in Beijing in the north and ends in Hangzhou in the south, running through Hebei, Tianjin, Shandong, Jiangsu and Zhejiang and spanning across the Haihe, Yellow, Huaihe, Yangtze and Qingtangjiang rivers. It was the golden waterway that once connected China's southern areas with the north.

Jade used in the Tang Dynasty fell into five categories – ritual, ornamental, decorative, utilitarian and Buddhist ware. Ritual jade ware mainly featured belt ornaments, also known as *daiban*, which were ornamental plates embedded in the waist belts of official robes. There was a rigid belt-using system in the Tang Dynasty, which stipulated that jade belts were the most noble and exclusive to emperors, princes and officials above the third rank. Ritual jade also included group ornaments tied at the waist and *guis* and *bis* used in sacrifices. Ornamental jade ware included items such as hairpins, *buyaos* (a head-dress that was inserted just beneath a hair bun), combs and phoenix-like ornaments. Decorative jade ware was mainly animal-shaped, and utilitarian ware included cups, boxes and incense burners. Buddhist jade wares mainly included figures of the Buddha and flying apsaras.

Ingeniously designed, jade ware in the Tang Dynasty boasted diverse shapes, exquisite craftsmanship, rich connotations and

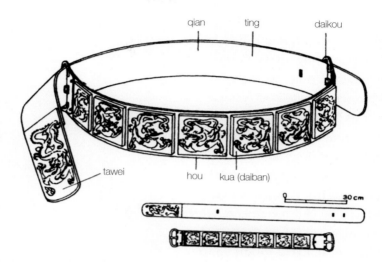

qian   ting   daikou

tawei   hou   kua (daiban)

30 cm

Names of the different parts of a jade belt

a unique style especially suitable for decoration. The new jade ware incorporated colorful cultural content, such as belt ornaments symbolizing official ranks and power, combs, flying apsaras with a foreign cultural flavor, as well as flower and bird patterns reflecting the beauty and romance of nature. These innovative jade wares and patterns pioneered the fashions of the time and provided inspiration for later periods as well.

The time of jade for kings had passed, but the concept of jade ware as a hierarchical token still

Li Zhi, Emperor Gaozong of the Tang Dynasty, wears a jade belt.

had a strong influence during the Tang Dynasty. The jade belt ornament was the typical example. Based on the number of ornamental rings on the belt, the belt ornaments fell into categories such as "thirteen-ornament belts" and "nine-ornament belts." The ornamental rings on official robes were mostly odd in number, symbolizing different official ranks. The belt ornaments were typically square or rectangular or close to a full moon shape, and some of them were even gold-rimmed. These ornaments generally had carved patterns of humans, animals, flowers and birds; most of the carved human figures were dressed in Tartar costume, showing a distinctive feature of the western regions. The jade plate with Huteng dance patterns, excavated from the cemetery

Jade plate with design of a Tartar man dancing Huteng, Tang Dynasty
Made of white jade, this rectangular plate bears the image of a man dancing Huteng. The dancer has long curly hair, a prominent nose, deep set eyes and a smiling face, which displays a strong flavor of the western regions.

of Zhaoling in Liquan County of Shaanxi Province, was an ornament on a belt. The plate features a Tartar man gracefully dancing Huteng – he has long, curly hair, a prominent nose, deep-set eyes, and a smiling face, which displayed a strong flavor of the western regions. The practice of using jade as a symbol of official status in imperial courts was followed until the Qing Dynasty.

Court ladies playing chess, Tang Dynasty
The ladies in the Tang Dynasty imperial court portrayed in the picture have small jade combs inserted in their hair, both beautiful and feminine.

Just as jade belt ornaments were exclusive to noble men in the palaces of the Tang Dynasty, ornamental jade ware such as combs were exclusive to ladies at court. The latter, typically having patterns of blooming flowers and flying birds, created a beauty of liveliness and gracefulness. Noble women in the Tang Dynasty inserted several small combs in their hair leaving the comb backs outside, which was a unique style. A beautiful jade comb from the tomb of the Shuiqiu Family (late Tang Dynasty) located in Lin'an, Hangzhou, Zhejiang, is 14.5 cm long and 5.7 cm wide, with both sides carved patterns of flowers and birds. The comb is full of vitality, and is an outstanding example of the jade combs of the Tang Dynasty.

The Tang Dynasty also saw the beginnings of jade ware related to Buddhism. Jade flying apsaras were one of its important expressive forms. The flying apsaras, or "gods of fragrance" in Chinese, were described in Buddhism as gods who were good at both playing music and dancing, picking fragrant dews of flowers, sending flowers and fragrance to the world, and bringing good luck to humans. When Buddhism was introduced to China, it was quickly combined with traditional Chinese culture and further developed into a distinctive Chinese form of Buddhism. The jade flying apsaras made in the Tang Dynasty had naked upper bodies and wore long skirts or loose trousers, raising both arms, holding flower branches in their hands and twisting both legs, giving a very romantic appearance.

The Tang Dynasty was an extremely brilliant period in Chinese civilization. As the center of international trade and

Flying apsara made of grey jade, Tang Dynasty
This kind-looking flying apsara has a graceful carriage. Dressed in a long robe, she wears a ribbon on her shoulders and flies in the clouds.

Suanni: The fifth son of the legendary dragon. Suannis are ferocious beasts that look like lions. Their images are generally found sitting on incense burners.

cultural communication, the Tang Dynasty spread Chinese culture widely, and also absorbed cultural and artistic fruits of Central and West Asia. Jade culture of the Tang Dynasty was flexible and open, as it not only inherited excellent national traditions, but also integrated parts of foreign cultures. From the jade ware of the Tang Dynasty, we can see such artistic images as lions, *suannis*, Tartars, and typical Tartar musical instruments, as well as flowers carved with thin lines and shapes simulating gold and silver ware of the western regions.

In 1970, an agate cup with an antelope head was unearthed from a kiln of the Tang Dynasty located in Hejia village, Xi'an, Shaanxi Province. Made of rare red onyx, the cup has distinct layers and a bright color. The antelope head looks lively, with two eye-catching strong horns. A dragon mouth-shaped gold lid that may be moved covers the antelope's snout. The shape of the cup is similar to the famous Persian rhyton. The earliest beast head-shaped cup known to have been used in Greece in the fifteenth century BC was a rhyton. It was considered sacred as it was funnel shaped and was used to pour sacred wine. The rhyton was later passed to Central Asia and West Asia, and eventually China. This unique agate cup was not only a superb representative of ware from the Tang Dynasty, but also an important cultural artifact resulting from the cross-fertilization of eastern and western cultures.

While directly influenced by culture of the western regions, the Tang Dynasty also exported traditional Chinese culture to other countries. This made Chinese culture flourish further and become integrated into other countries' cultures, and laid the initial foundation for the international study of jade culture conducted in modern times.

An agate cup with antelope head, Tang Dynasty.

Jade Ware in the Song Dynasty

In Chinese cultural history, the Song Dynasty (960–1279) was a very special period as emperors advocated ruling the world by emphasizing civil matters. As a result of the policy of "preferring the pen to the sword," abandoning military careers and reading more books became the fashion of the time, which led to extraordinary cultural and artistic achievements. Even Emperor Huizong (r. 1100–1125) of the Song Dynasty was very good at writing and drawing and had discriminating artistic taste. His appreciation exerted a profound impact on jade ware of the Song Dynasty.

Major jade ware categories in the Song Dynasty included court jade, such as belts used in official robes and crowns; antique jade such as *bis*, rings and incense burners; ornamental items such as hairpins, combs, necklaces, finger rings and bracelets, as well as pendants of various designs, such as flowers, birds, dragons, boys, animals, fruits and auspicious beasts. There were also articles used in everyday life such as bowls, cups, boxes and stoves; jade used in writing such as ink stones, small containers of water for ink stones, brushes, brush washers, brush racks, paperweights and seals. As for some animal-shaped artwork made by carving in the round, such as sleeping goat, mythical beast, and double crane-shaped designs, they were used for decoration or as paperweights. Utilizing the best quality materials and exquisitely carved and polished, jade craftsmanship integrated multiple techniques, including incision and hollow cutting. Involving a wide variety of subjects for decoration, the patterns on the jade ware were mostly flowers and birds in pairs, which rendered a balanced artistic effect, and embodied the innovative spirit of jade culture in the Song Dynasty. This set

Jade incense burner with handles in the form of beasts with dragon and cloud patterns, Song Dynasty.

the scene for the development of jade decorative artwork in the following Yuan, Ming and Qing dynasties.

The aesthetic style of pursuing nature and rough carving in the Song Dynasty resulted in simple and bold jade-working techniques, as well as more emphasis on unified, clear and complete overall effects with detailed carving not particularly intended as real images. Deep and strong lines made the artistic images appear vigorous and harmonious. The use of rough carving in the Song Dynasty imbued many small-sized artifacts with certain spiritual forces and made them look exquisitely pretty. Plain shapes also gave seemingly simple ware deep meanings. For example, the patterns combining flowers and birds appeared peaceful, fresh and natural, and contained infinite vitality, showing the people's great passion for life.

The Northern Song Dynasty saw the first interest in collections in Chinese history. As Emperor Huizong (r. 1100–1126) was very fond of antiques, particularly antique jade, and a great number of antique jade artifacts were unearthed in the period, the Song people, both at court and in civil society, developed greater interest in antique jade and collecting antique jade. This also resulted in the discovery of more antique jade and thus added new content to the jade ware of the Song Dynasty and later dynasties. Antique jade of the Song Dynasty mainly included *bis*, rings, and stoves. A double beast-shaped stove with handles, decorated with cloud and dragon patterns from the Song Dynasty is in the Palace Museum collection. Made of grey jade and round-shaped, it is hollow inside with a wide mouth and ringed feet. This is far from the only antique jade that both simulated ancient ware shapes and incorporated prevailing patterns at that time. Antique-style jade ware of the Song Dynasty was not simply imitating those of ancient times, but integrated styles of the time, which not only showed the nostalgic feelings of the Song people, but also brought something new to Chinese jade culture.

Jade ware in the Song Dynasty was more secularized and displayed a stronger sense of life than in the Tang Dynasty. With the rapid growth of the urban economy and expansion of an emerging middle class, it was inevitable that jade ware would serve the public. This phenomenon first appeared in the Tang Dynasty and became the main trend for jade development in the Song and Yuan dynasties. Jade ware before the Wei and Jin dynasties, other than for decorative purposes, served primitive religions, symbolized hierarchies or advocated ethics. Fantastic dragons, kylins and phoenixes, as well as mysterious cloud, thunder and grain patterns, constituted a conceptual world that went far beyond reality. Occult jade ware with special meanings had long been monopolized by the ruling class and could not be understood and accepted by the masses. To cater for new requirements in this new situation, jade ware became secularized.

People abandoned the practice of making jade ware solely relying on fantasy and adopted the most common subjects in daily life for artistic creation. With the development of a commodity economy, civil jade carving thrived, with its major consumers including the nouveaux riche class who generally were not so well educated but were keen about jade ware, in addition to senior officials, nobles and refined scholars. Against such a background, the Song Dynasty created a lot of secularized jade ware that met public demands, such as those with subjects like "Flourishing offspring," "Successive years of surplus' and "Boy holding lotus."

Jade boy holding lotus, Song Dynasty
Made of white-yellow jade, a boy, dressed in summer clothes and loose pants, crosses his legs, with a lotus in his left hand and a silk ball in his right. The image evokes the people's good wishes for a better life.

"Boy holding lotus" was a dominant theme at that time and is closely associated with the Buddhist story "The girl with a deer mother gave birth to a lotus." The story is as follows: Once upon a time, on the immortal mountain in Benares of the western regions lived an immortal named Fan Zhi who often urinated on mountain stones. After licking his urine, a female deer got pregnant and gave birth to a girl. The girl, brought up by Fan Zhi, later married the king as his second wife. Afterwards, she gave birth to a lotus with 1,000 leaves and on each of the leaves was a boy. These boys were brought up and became useful people who were extremely strong and powerful.

Then came the idea that children who wore "Boy holding lotus" jade pendants would be healthy and talented, and adults who carried the jade pendants would give birth to boys. Such jade ware expressed people's good wishes for a happy life.

While growing secularized, jade ware in the Song Dynasty also showed an obvious trend of becoming more artistic. This was not only the inevitable result of the cultural and artistic development in the Song Dynasty, but also reflected the new connotations the intellectual class incorporated into jade culture. The Song Dynasty saw great progress in jade wares with flower patterns that appeared since the Tang Dynasty. As the Song people often relied on nature to express their personal ideals and national values, nature became the subject for people to convey their inner feelings, and natural scenery became the outer expression of human emotions and spirits. Hence, some

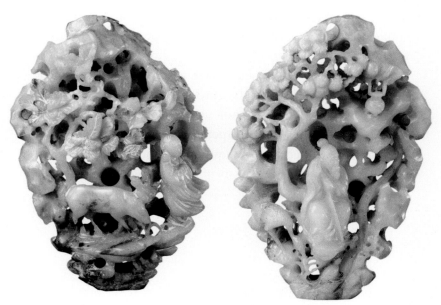

Grey jade *shanzi* with carved figures, Song Dynasty

relatively fixed symbolism developed. For instance, the plum blossom symbolized unyielding character, bamboo represented moral integrity and lotus meant freedom from vulgarity. Affected by the ideology and cultural environment of the period, jade ware in the Song Dynasty described the beauty of life with fresh, graceful shapes and romantic style, rather than praising real life through the bold style of Tang Dynasty jade ware. The pure and noble character typical of scholars made jade ware of the Song Dynasty appear fresh and natural and gave them a beautiful sense of peace.

The grey jade *shanzi* with carved figures that is currently in the Palace Museum collection is a beautiful jade carved drawing. This piece is in the shape of an irregular ellipse, with a pattern integrating round carving, hollow carving and fretwork techniques. It depicts an elderly man and his two servants, as well as beautiful scenery including mountains, flowing brooks, pine trees, peonies, tortoises and cranes, deer and incense burners. The whole artwork, with vivid patterns and auspicious implications, was the most exquisite one of its kind from the Song Dynasty.

Jade ware of the Song Dynasty, while inheriting strengths of jade ware in the Tang Dynasty, absorbed useful elements from the Liao and Jin dynasties, thus integrating real life and art. Song Dynasty jade, with its superb carving techniques, vivid flower and bird patterns and unique antique jade wares, had far-reaching influence upon jade ware of later periods.

Jade Ware in the Liao Dynasty

The Liao Dynasty (907–1125) was a local regime founded by the Qidan (Khitan) people who lived in the Liaohe River Basin in northeast China. Jade ware in the Liao Dynasty featured a small number of items including belts, pendants, containers and Buddhist ware. Hotan jade was favored in this period and was used together with gold, silver and precious stones. Jade ware in the Liao Dynasty also boasted diverse shapes: animal-shaped artifacts had natural and realistic images rather than exaggerated and strange shapes; containers for daily use were decorated with common and popular subjects rather than complicated patterns. The plain and realistic style was typical of jade ware in the Liao Dynasty.

If the Western and Eastern Han dynasties could be considered the period that saw the first peak in the use of Hotan jade, the Liao Dynasty witnessed another peak. Ornaments in the Liao

This 14.8-cm-long jade group pendant was unearthed from the tomb of a princess of the State of Chen in the Liao Dynasty, located in Inner Mongolia.

Dynasty mostly used Hotan "sheep-fat" jade. Using extremely strict selection procedures, the jade materials used were all pure and flawless, as white as snow and as softly luminescent as grease. Several animal- and tool-shaped white jade pendants, unearthed from the tomb of the Princess of the State of Chen in the Liao Dynasty in Inner Mongolia in 1986, may be regarded as typical representatives of jade of the Liao Dynasty. Among them is a set of dragon-phoenix shaped pendants made of Hotan jade and composed of six pieces of exquisite dragon, phoenix and flying fish-shaped jade ornaments and gold chains. When unearthed, it was placed on top of the princess's chest. Another set of unique tool-shaped pendants, with each piece measuring 5.8 cm long and 8.2 cm wide, were also made of white Hotan jade and consisted of a knife, gimlet, file, scoop, scissors and bodkin-shaped jade tools, a piece of lotus-like jade plate and gold chains that were connected with each other. It was placed on the princess' gold belt when unearthed and was presumably the pendant carried by the princess when she was alive.

A tool-design pendant unearthed from the tomb of a princess of the State of Chen in the Liao Dynasty, located in Inner Mongolia.

Artistic subjects related to Buddhist jade ware from the Liao Dynasty included three categories: flying apsaras, the Capricorn and the Garuda. Flying apsaras were an extension of jade ware of the Tang Dynasty, and the other two were innovative forms. The Capricorn was a divine beast with a dragon head, fish body and two wings. It was also called a fish-dragon and was a new image created with the introduction of Buddhism. In Indian mythology, the Capricorn was an animal with a long nose, sharp teeth, and a fish body and tail. Regarded as the essence of the river and root of life, it often appeared in ancient Indian carvings and drawings. With the passage of time, the Capricorn pattern was integrated with Chinese folktales and developed into the fish-dragon pattern that became a prevailing decoration in periods after the Tang Dynasty. The Garuda was also introduced into China with Buddhism, and most of the carvings adopted the round-carving technique. The arms and the Garuda's head were highlighted in the front of the carving, with two extending wings on both sides and a beautiful fantail at the back. In Indian mythology, the Garuda was a strange creature, half-human and half-bird, and referred to as the golden-winged bird when introduced to China. Feeding on dragons and extremely powerful, it belonged to a protector of the Buddhist Dharma and was believed to be capable of bringing good luck and happiness to the people.

Grey jade Capricorn ornament,
Liao Dynasty
This Capricorn, made of grey-white jade, holds a ball in its mouth and is ready to fly.

Grey jade Garuda (divine bird), Liao Dynasty

Jade Ware in the Jin Dynasty

The Jin Dynasty (1115–1234) was a feudal dynasty founded by the Jurchen people who lived in the northeastern part of China. "Spring river" and "Autumn mountain" jade were the most distinctive among jade ware of the Jin Dynasty. The former theme referred to falcons catching wild geese in the green grass

Picture of a hunting scene
This image portrays five Khitan men ready to go hunting in the spring. One of them rolls his sleeves, the other four hold a falcon, shoes, a *qin* (an ancient Chinese musical instrument), and a bow.

Grey jade ornament with design of a falcon capturing a
swan (spring river jade), Jin Dynasty
This piece of jade was carved with a diving falcon chasing
a swan hiding in louts leaves.

in the spring, and the latter to hunting tigers and deer in the mountains in the autumn, reflecting the hunting scene of the Jin people. The unique jade pendants with flower and bird patterns of the Jurchen people, while retaining their own features and inheriting Liao Dynasty traditions, displayed a unique artistic style influenced by the jade-carving techniques of the Song Dynasty. Jade ware in the Jin Dynasty boasted rich content and was in no way inferior to that of the Song Dynasty. In addition to the flower and bird images that were most common in jade ware of the Song Dynasty, pictures using the "Spring river" and "Autumn mountain" themes were also added with appropriate proportions and integrating both images and spirits, thus giving the jade ware great artistic value.

The "Spring river" jade reflected the hunting life of the Khitan and Jurchen peoples. The Gyr Falcon (*haidongqing*) was the

Double deer-shaped jade ornament (autumn mountain jade), Jin Dynasty
This whole piece of jade is triangular, with two little deer, a buck and a doe, in the center. One of the deer is turning around, and the other is stretching its neck and walking. Above the deer is a wild goose.

major participant in hunting and considered to be a divine bird by the northern ethnic group. The "Spring river" jade described the scene when the *haidongqing* captured swans or wild geese. The scene was specially recorded in some ancient literature: in the early days of the first month in the Chinese Lunar Calendar, the emperor would lead a hunting party towards the banks of the Yazi River in Changchun, northeastern China. After dozens of days of traveling, they arrived and set up an encampment. They set out at dawn to hunt and returned at dusk. The emperor watched the prey's actions from a distant, high place, and once he found geese, he would raise a flag to tell his followers and beat a drum to scare the geese. When the geese flew into the sky, the attendants would present the *haidongqing* to him and the emperor would free the falcon to let it chase the geese. As soon as the *haidongqing* caught the goose, it would immediately attack its head. The attendants then killed the goose with a specially made gimlet and cut the head to feed the *haidongqing*.

Jade ornament with a Paradise Flycatcher perching among flowers, Jin Dynasty

The emperor would then entertain his ministers when he got the first goose. Hunting would typically last until the end of spring. The "Spring river" jade, with a hunting scene as the theme, showed the exciting moment when the *haidongqing* captured the swan. The lotus and grass swaying with the wind, the swans in panic trying to hide from the attack, as well as the smart and ferocious *haidongqing*, all look vivid and lively. The tableau, perfectly combining both scene and spirit, was a miniature scene of the hunting life and culture of the nomadic people in the northeastern part of China.

In the autumn, the Jurchen people went into the mountains to hunt. When late autumn came, emperors would lead parties to hunt tigers and deer in mountains, and this constituted the major subject for the "Autumn mountain" jade. Some of the carved pictures depict both tigers and deer in mountains; some showed pairs of roaming deer or tigers hiding in trees; most showed deer in thick forests with mountains and oak trees. The "Autumn mountain" jade displayed a less violent picture than the "Spring river" jade and instead highlighted the beautiful grassland scenery typical of the northeastern areas, consisting of wild forests and various beasts living in harmony. This reflected the Jurchen people's wishes for peace.

Jade ornamental pendants of the Jurchen People in the Jin Dynasty developed well in this period. Flower and bird patterns were the most common, with popular subjects involving Paradise Flycatchers (*shoudai* bird), tortoise nests and lotus leaves. Examples of such artifacts were unearthed from a Jin Dynasty tomb in Wangzuo Village, Fengtai District, Beijing. Among them was a pendant with patterns of a Paradise Flycatcher perched among flowers, 6 cm in diameter and made of white jade. The picture looks beautiful and has novel implications. The Paradise Flycatcher symbolized happiness and longevity as the *shou* in its name sounds like the Chinese character "*shou*" or longevity. The Paradise Flycatcher among flowers implied infinite happiness and long life. Another jade pendant with patterns of tortoise nests, 10 cm long and 7 cm wide, was carved out of grey jade. The pattern, suggesting two tortoises sitting on lotus leaves, was called "tortoise travel" in ancient times, implying good fortune and longevity.

Jade Ware in the Yuan Dynasty

The Yuan Dynasty (1276–1368) ruled over a unified multi-ethnic country founded by the Mongols in 1279. In this period, jade ware workshops run by the government were set up in Dadu and Hangzhou to specialize in producing jade to be used in the imperial court. Meanwhile, private jade workshops flourished as well. Jade artisans of the Yuan Dynasty, while inheriting and developing the superb enchasing techniques of the Song and Jin dynasties, applied relief techniques proficiently, too, with patterns mainly including flowers and birds, mountains and rivers, dragon-tigers and marine beasts. Some jade ware also featured a unique rough style, as was shown in the fact that the jade's surface was carved and polished carefully and exquisitely, while the inner surface or base were coarsely polished.

Jade working in the Yuan Dynasty fell into two parts: coarse cutting and refined carving. The strongly carved coarse jade ware appeared bold and integrated antique features well; it serves as the best portrait of the bold and unconstrained character of the northern people. When building the capital city Beijing, Kublai Khan (r. 1260–1294), the first emperor of the Yuan Dynasty spared no expense in having a huge wine bowl made specifically for drinking wine at banquets, thus satisfying his need for drinking and recreation. The wine bowl, called "Extra large jade bowl of Dushan" is 70 cm tall, 55 cm deep, and 135–182 cm in diameter, with the maximum circumference being 493 cm. It weighs 3,500 kg and could hold 30-plus *shi* (an ancient unit of volume) of wine. Grey and black, the jade wine bowl had carved patterns of the surging sea as well as vivid flood dragons, marine horses, flying fish, hippopotamuses and trumpet shells in various shapes. Several hundred years later, inscriptions were carved on the inner surface of the jade ware containing three poems of Emperor Qianlong (r. 1735–1795) and a summary of the experiences of the extra large jade bowl.

This wine bowl was placed in the Hall of Vast Cold on the top of Longevity Hill in Beihai Park in Beijing, and then moved to several places, including the Zhenwu Temple (later renamed the Shibo Temple) on the southwest side of Donghua Gate of the Forbidden City after the Hall of Vast Cold was destroyed. Kublai Khan first used it for drinking wine at banquets, later it was changed into a Buddhist alms bowl in the late Ming Dynasty and finally used as a dish urn for Taoists. In 1749, Emperor Qianlong bought the giant bowl at an extremely high price and placed it in the Yuweng Pavilion in front of the Hall to Receive the Light in Beihai Park, where it has been kept to this day. It is the earliest large-sized jade carving known so far and is a typical example of Chinese jade ware integrating superb working techniques including "choosing jade according to raw materials"

Extra large jade bowl of Dushan, Yuan Dynasty

Jade incense burner, Yuan Dynasty
This was unearthed from the site of Dadu city in
Xicheng District, Beijing

and "carving according to jade," and had a very appropriate application of color. With a plain shape and bold decorative patterns, it was exquisitely carved with superb workmanship and shows a sense of mystery and romance. The extra large jade bowl is a piece of precious epoch-making artwork.

The Yuan Dynasty saw some progression in the shapes of jade ware: the stove top is one example. The jade furnace top, unearthed from the site of Dadu city in Beijing, was made of grey jade and measures 3.5 cm tall and 3.7 cm wide. With multiple layers of patterns carved with openwork techniques, it depicts a bittern on a lotus, which implies "successive successes." The jade ware was exquisitely polished but has a rough inner surface, and this also reflects jade making in the Yuan Dynasty.

Jade Ware in the Ming Dynasty

With the practice of jade appreciation prevailing in the Ming Dynasty (1368–1644), jade ware developed quickly and jade carving improved. Many jade artifacts integrated decoration,

Zhu Yojun, Emperor Shenzong (r.1067–1085) of the Ming Dynasty, wears a jade belt.

appreciation and practical use. The amount of ritual jade decreased dramatically and jade used in daily life increased gradually and extended into every aspect of life. Ritual jade at this time included the auspicious *bi* with orderly dot patterns, as well as belt ornaments and group pendants with magnificent designs. Ornamental jade mostly consisted of pendants and plates as well as belt hooks worn by the people. Carrying jade also became a common custom of ordinary citizens. Jade was not only worn but also stitched on clothes. There was an even greater number of auspicious jade decorations and precious jade ware for daily use. In addition, many innovative items appeared as well, mostly being incense burners, tools used in writing and tea ware. With shapes inherited from the traditions of the Song Dynasty, they had patterns like flowers, fruits, insects, birds and beasts, which were carved more vividly and carefully.

A developed commodity economy and increasingly expanding middle class in the Ming Dynasty resulted in greater demand for jade ware, and the jade carving industry thrived. Both public and private workshops made jade ware as exquisitely as they could to meet market demand. Superb white Hotan jade, refined craftsmanship as well as colorful shapes and patterns led to the creation of numerous fine wares. Meanwhile, the embedding technique combining jade and gold and silver jewelry reached its peak. Royal families, senior officials and nobles were not just content with jade itself,

Leaf-shaped jade ornament with a gold cicada, Ming Dynasty
This piece features a transparent and thin jade leaf on which stands a vivid gold cicada.

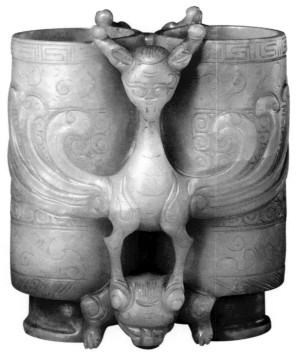

Grey jade nuptial wine cup, Ming Dynasty
Decorated with grain and cloud patterns, it consists
of two connected cylinders and round legs. An eagle
and a bear sit between the two cylinders. Newlyweds
would use these nuptial wine cups to drink wine on their
wedding day.

so they integrated jade with gold and silver and embedded jade
in gold and silver ware. Typical items from this period included
a jade cup with gold saucer and jade hairpin with embedded
gold unearthed from the Dingling tomb from the Ming Dynasty.
Although jade ware with embedded gold or jade has had a long
history in China, gold and jade mixed ware did not appear until
the Ming Dynasty.

Zheng He (1371–1435) made a journey to the western seas
in the early Ming Dynasty. Maritime trade was extraordinarily
prosperous at that time, and while China exported lots of

Jade cup with gold saucer, Ming Dynasty.

porcelain and silk, it received much precious jewelry in return. Various precious stones were unearthed from the tomb of emperors from the Ming Dynasty as well as tombs of royal princes and nobles, including rubies, sapphires, emeralds and opals. Most of them were imported to China from Sri Lanka. The jades unearthed from the Dingling tomb, one of the Thirteen Ming Tombs located in Changping District, Beijing, were mostly embedded with gold and jewelry, with the jade cup with gold saucer and gold hairpin with embedded jade being the most exquisite. The *yuanbao* ingot-shaped cup is 11.5 cm tall and made of grey-white jade, paired with a gold saucer embedded with rubies and sapphires. The cup suggests long life and infinite happiness. The gold hairpin is about 13.5 cm long and surmounted with a flawless white jade plate. The

Jade hairpin embedded with gold, Ming Dynasty.

plate itself was carved into a flower-shaped Chinese character "*shou*," surrounded by gold embedded with precious stones, opals and pearls.

Jade artisans enjoyed a higher status in the Ming Dynasty thanks to the flourishing jade ware industry. Previously, professional jade artisans contributed greatly to the brilliant ancient Chinese jade culture, but they were not well respected and were not awarded corresponding social status, living towards the bottom of the societal structure. According to the system lasting from the Shang and Zhou dynasties to the Yuan Dynasty, jade artisans had always been under government administration and registered separately. They worked for rulers all year long, while earning a menial income to support their families. Moreover, their occupation as jade artisans was passed on from generation to generation without change. The extremely low social status of these craftsmen greatly

Grey jade kettle with design of boys playing, Ming Dynasty
The image of boys playing was carved on both sides of the
kettle's body. The kettle has a lid with a lion-shaped knob.
The two Chinese characters "Zigang", are inscribed beneath
the base of the lion, and cannot be seen unless the lid and
knob are separated.

dampened the enthusiasm of jade artisans for production. With
a loosening of restrictions on personal freedom in the Ming
Dynasty, jade workers enjoyed correspondingly improved
social status.

There were several major jade-making bases including
Beijing, Nanjing, Hangzhou and Suzhou in the Ming Dynasty;
Suzhou was the most famous of these. The period also saw
superb craftsmanship and numerous eminent jade artisans. Lu
Zigang was one of them. As a jade craftsman in Suzhou during
the reigns of emperors Jiajing and Wanli of the Ming Dynasty,
he was very well known both at court and in society at large.
Creating numerous superb, elegant artworks, he was the pioneer

who first carved his name on jade ware. Inspired by Ming Dynasty scholars who wrote their names on their calligraphy or paintings, he often inscribed the characters "Lu Zigang" or "Zigang," either in *zhuan* script or *kai*-script, on the bottom or sides of his creations. This reflected the prosperity of jade ware production in the Ming Dynasty, and served as a symbol of high-quality jade ware, making inscriptions somewhat equal to trademarks. As for Lu Zigang's practice of carving names on jade, there is a folktale:

The emperor wanted Lu Zigang to make a jade kettle for him but would not allow him to leave his name on it. Lu Zigang, who always refused to made jade ware without carving his name on it, had to accept the imperial edict because disobeying the order would have had him killed. He thought it over and finally carved a horse on the kettle. After finishing it, he presented it to the emperor, who found no inscriptions on the exquisitely made jade work after careful examination and was very satisfied. However, one of his ministers finally discovered something wrong: Lu Zigang had carved two characters "Zigang" inside the horse's ear. Although the emperor did not punish him, Lu Zigang offended the emperor anyway.

With increasing popular interest in everyday life people and the greater demand for jade, the Ming Dynasty saw a lot of jade ware reflecting folk customs and public beliefs that included customs, legends, religious beliefs and auspicious concepts. Folk culture at this time, deeply rooted in society and with a profound national foundation, was gradually appreciated by royal families, aristocrats and scholars, and thus frequently appeared on jade ware designs. Auspicious patterns prevailing in the society included those such as the "Gods of Fortune, Prosperity and Longevity," the "Eight Immortals," "Carp Jumping the Dragon Gate," and "Children at Play." These were found even on jade ware in the imperial palace. Jade artwork in the

Jade ornament with "Wang Xizhi with his favorite geese,"
Ming Dynasty.

Ming Dynasty, those used both in court and society, displayed a sense of ordinary life.

We can see the strong sense of life embodied in the jade ware of the Ming Dynasty from the two jade carvings collected at the Palace Museum, with one being a jade ornament from the Ming Dynasty called "Wang Xizhi with his favorite geese." Made of grey jade, it is 10 cm long and rectangular-shaped. Wang Xizhi (321–379) was an outstanding calligrapher in the Eastern Jin Dynasty. It is said he got tips on how to use brushes from geese swimming and hence loved geese very much. He learnt that a Taoist living the mountains had a flock of geese, so he went to have a look and offered to buy the geese at a high price. The Taoist happened to like Wang's calligraphy and offered to exchange his geese for Wang's calligraphic work *Dao De Jing*. Wang accepted enthusiastically. This piece of jade work was based on the folktale and carved with relief technique. An elderly Wang Xizhi watches the goose raising its head and tail, and a boy gently holds the goose. The picture expresses rich content with smooth lines. The other carving is a piece of jade called "Tibetans on treasure boat." Made of grey jade, it is 11.5 cm tall, 29.5 cm long and 8 cm wide. The boat, carved to look like it is made of wood, carries nine people, all of whom are holding something, a rhinoceros horn, *ruyi*, silk ball or *reishi*, and one is holding paddles to row the boat. The people are dressed in different clothes and look like Tibetans. A lion and an elephant stand in the front of the boat, there is a big dragon-eared flat bottle in the middle and a towering ancient pine with two cranes standing on it in the rear of the boat. These Tibetans and the items they hold all have their meanings. For instance, the rhinoceros horn and silk ball are precious treasures and represent wealth; *reishi* and cranes imply longevity; "bottle" sounds like the Chinese character *"ping,"* which means safety. The artwork implies multiple auspicious words, such as "Tibetans offer treasure," "Immortals offering their birthday wishes," "Elephant brings peace," "All wishes come true" and "Longevity and wealth." The practice of expressing feelings through auspicious words began in the Song Dynasty and prevailed in the Ming Dynasty, and this piece of jade ware is the best reflection of the folk custom that "pictures always have their auspicious meanings."

Collecting antique jade became even more popular in the Ming Dynasty than in the Song Dynasty. Particularly with the growth of capitalism in the late Ming Dynasty, industrial and commercial economies developed and the middle class rose. Some rich merchants, keen to show off their interest in art and pretentious artistic talent, competed in buying famous calligraphic works, paintings, and antiques, including jade. Triggered by this market demand, jade craftsmen made a vast amount of artifacts to cater to these interests and made profits.

Jade Ware in the Qing Dynasty

Production department:
First set up by Emperor Kangxi of the Qing Dynasty, directly under the Office of the Imperial Household, it was responsible for all sorts of paraphernalia used in the imperial palace. The department, at its height, comprised forty-two workshops, each of which drew ingenious craftsmen from across the country. The artifacts they made covered every aspect of the daily lives of those in the imperial court of the Ming Dynasty, ranging from food and clothes to ware for use and recreation. It was thus called the "Various Technology Workshop."

The Qing Dynasty (1644–1911) was founded by the Manchu people and was China's last feudal dynasty. In ancient Chinese society, the preferences of the rulers typically established the tastes of wider society. Jade ware was greatly cherished by the Emperor Qianlong (r.1736–1795). Shortly after the Qing Dynasty was founded, a production department was set up in the court, specializing in making jade for royalty. Emperor Qianlong invested more manpower, materials and money in jade working than any other emperor in Chinese history. Meanwhile, as Qianlong loved collecting antique jade, many of his ministers presented jade artifacts to him, which resulted in collecting antique jade reaching its peak in society. Most of the 10,000 pieces of antique jade ware surviving from the Qing Dynasty that are presently in the Palace Museum were collected by Emperor Qianlong. He not only collected jade, but also appreciated and appraised jade ware himself. Every time he acquired a precious jade, he wrote a poem of praise. Indeed, nearly 800 of Qianlong's poems were about jade ware. If he found any piece of antique jade ware roughly made, he would order the production department to further process it. Emperor Qianlong particularly paid attention to jade-ware production in the court and inquired about the allocation of labor in the jade production department. Under the influence of Qianlong, many court painters designed and painted jade carvings, which greatly enhanced the artistic appearance of jade ware. Every jade artifact in the palace during the Qing Dynasty was splendid, and this could be largely attributed to the efforts of Emperor Qianlong.

Emperor Qianlong loved jade, and nearly 800 of his poems were written in praise of jade ware.

Jade ware produced during this period can be divided into that of the early, middle and late periods of the Dynasty. Jades in the early period were small in number and basically continued the shapes of those in the late Ming Dynasty; the middle Qing Dynasty, including the successive reigns of emperors Kangxi (r. 1662–1722), Yongzheng (r. 1722–1736), Qianlong, and Jiaqing (r. 1795–1820), saw a rapid development of jade ware. The jade ware mainly fell into the following categories: ritual items, such as quills, hats, and court beads used by officials of the Qing Dynasty, imperial seals as well as jade *gui, bi* and *qing* used

Green jade seal "*Huangdi fengtian zhibao*"("Becoming the Emperor by the grace of the gods"), Qing Dynasty.

The four treasures of the study, which were necessities placed on the emperor's imperial table and used to review written reports. The picture shows a jade brush, jade brush pot, jade ink rest, jade arm rest and jade paper weight.

A hair ornament used by women in the Qing Dynasty. Made of white jade that is smooth and without veins, this piece was embedded with flowers and grass made of colorful precious stones on both ends.

in sacrifices; ornamental items, such as belt hooks, belt buttons and thumb-rings used by men, and hairpins and pendants used by women; decorative pieces, such as *shanzi, ruyi*, antique-style jade as well as animals, plants and figures made with round carving techniques; tools used in daily life, such as incense burners, flower bottles and food containers of various sorts; in addition, there were tools used in writing and religious rituals. Jade ware in the late Qing Dynasty mainly served the people, and mostly consisted of practical items.

After the Emperor Qianlong had quelled a rebellion in the western areas, jade produced from Xinjiang was imported to Central China on an unprecedented large scale.

Sitting Buddha made of Hotan jade, Qing Dynasty
The jade Buddha, with the appropriate proportions, looks kind and serious. It was superbly carved by craftsmen in the middle and late Qing Dynasty.

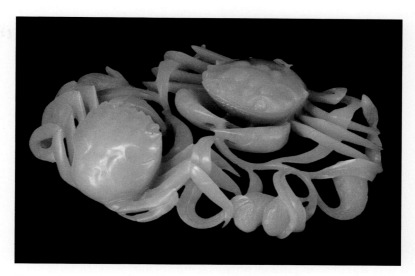

Pair of crab-shaped paperweights made of Hotan jade, Qing Dynasty.

From the twenty-fifth year of the reign of Emperor Qianlong (1760), 2,000 kilograms of Hotan jade was presented to the court annually, and more was extracted for special needs. Besides, Hotan jade was also heavily exploited at this time, and this produced enough raw material for the flourishing jade-working industry of the Qing Dynasty.

Both the shapes and patterns of jade ware in the Qing Dynasty, either in court or in civil society, reflected various aspects of life. Common shapes included calabashes, flowers, cabbages, goats, fish and crabs, which were closely related to daily life. Other designs included flowers and birds, mountains and rivers, human figures, boys at play, plum blossom and bamboos, the animal zodiacs, butterflies and mandarin ducks, which were close to nature, and also vivid and realistic.

A highly prosperous urban economy and the rapid expansion of the middle class in the Qing Dynasty led to the further expansion of services in jade ware, with more workshops producing jade, gradual increasing output and creating significant breakthroughs in jade-working techniques. These laid a material and social foundation for the further development of jade ware. Qing Dynasty jade ware not only inherited the excellent traditions of those in the former dynasties, but also integrated the artistic methods adopted in painting, carving and gold- and silver-smithing at that time. By perfectly combining such techniques as incision, round and relief carving, and enchasing, jade ware in the Qing Dynasty reached an extremely high standard, with unprecedentedly large numbers, diverse purposes, exquisite shapes, superb carvings and beautiful patterns. Jade ware made in the reign of Emperor Qianlong was the best of all the ware produced in the Qing Dynasty. Therefore, this particular period witnessed another peak in jade ware development following the Han Dynasty, and was a golden period that saw the culmination of all strengths of jade ware from previous dynasties.

It is no exaggeration to say that jade artisans in the Qing Dynasty had such superb craftsmanship it perhaps startled even the gods. These craftsmen not only created a large-sized jade carving named "Jade hill of Dayu regulating water" that could be crowned as one of the wonders in the world, but also could design jade ware following the form of the raw materials and transform waste into treasures. The jade ornament "Beauties standing under tung trees" was a typical example.

"Beauties standing under tung trees," presently in the Palace Museum in Beijing, is 15.5 cm tall, 25 cm wide and 10.8 cm deep It was made of Hotan jade from Xinjiang, with part of its outer surface tinted in orange. In the middle of the piece is a door composed of two half-moon-shaped parts and left half open. Both inside and outside the door stands a girl dressed in a long gown. One girl is holding flowers and the other is holding a box in both hands, and they look at each other through the

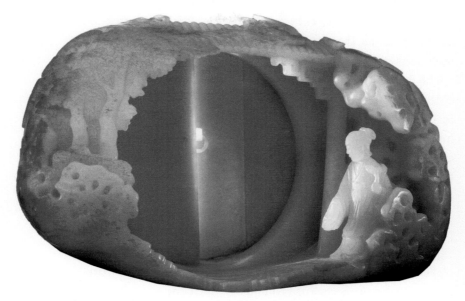

Jade ornament with images of beauties standing under tung trees, Qing Dynasty

opening. By taking advantage of the white color of the jade and orange color of the surface, rush tung trees, artificial hills consisting of piled stones, stone tables and stools were carved on the jade, displaying a beautiful scene typical of the gardens in the areas south of the Yangtze River. The base of the jade ware is flat and smooth, with the inscriptions of an "imperial topic" poem and an essay written by Emperor Qianlong. According to the inscription, jade artisans made the ornament in Suzhou in the thirty-eighth year of the reign of Qianlong (1773). It was originally a piece of waste jade left over from making a bowl, but was used by clever jade craftsmen who, based on its shape and color, ingeniously carved it into a precious artwork with extraordinary artistic value. So it is no wonder that Emperor Qianlong praised the jade artisans in Suzhou for their contribution that was equal or even greater than that of Bian

He who presented the *He Shi Bi*. This piece of jade ware may be listed among the great representatives of Chinese jade ware that impressed the world with its superb craftsmanship and ingenious use of materials.

The jade boulder sculptures of "Dayu regulating water," "Nine elders at Huichang," "Trip in Guanshan," and "Spring morning in Dantai" from the palace of the Qing Dynasty weigh from hundreds of *jin* (half a kilogram) to several tons. Each of these extremely large jade artworks undoubtedly represents a huge project, from material selection, design and drawing to carving and shaping. By successfully carving the jade into such exquisite artworks, craftsmen in the Qing Dynasty perfectly harnessed the power and beauty of the great empire and created a splendid chapter in the Chinese jade carving history. The boulder sculpture of "Dayu regulating water," the largest jade carved artwork in the world, best reflects this brilliant achievement.

The sculpture "Dayu regulating water," is 224 cm tall and 96 cm wide, weighs over 5,000 kilograms and is made of grey jade. In the carved design, there are high mountains and lofty peaks, a flowing spring and tumbling waterfalls, old trees and evergreen pines. On the steep cliffs are groups of people digging the mountain and moving stones. Some of them are chiseling stones, some shoveling sand and some piling stones. What a busy scene it is! There is an inscription of ten Chinese *zhuan* characters on the front of the boulder: "*Wu fu wu dai tang gu xi tian zi bao.*" On the lower part of the other side are six *zhuan* characters "*Ba zheng mao nian zhi bao,*" and on the upper part were inscriptions consisting of over 1,000 Chinese characters, with the contents including the "Seven-Character-In-A-Line poem," *Mileta Mountain jade-made picture of Dayu regulating water* and its notes. According to the inscription, the material of the jade boulder came from the Mileta Mountain, and the design came from a painting from the Song Dynasty that was

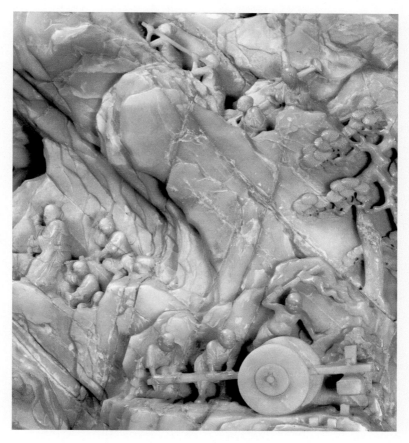

Jade hill of "Dayu regulating water," Qing Dynasty.

collected in the palace of the Qing Dynasty. Emperor Qianlong commissioned this sculpture to record his feats while praising the immortal contributions of Dayu in regulating the rivers. It is recorded that the piece of jade ware took jade-carving masters in Yangzhou of Jiangsu ten years to complete and was finally finished in the fifty-third year in the reign of Emperor Qianlong (1788). It has been kept in the Hall of Happiness and Longevity in the Forbidden City to this day. Investigations

Jade hill of "Dayu regulating water," Qing Dynasty.

Hotan jade bowl embedded with gold and precious stones, Qing Dynasty
Made of white and flawless jade, the bowl has a flower-shaped bottom. On the lower part of its outer surface are gold leaves and flowers embedded with red rubies, and on the inner surface are patterns of embedded gold leaves. The bowl, used in tea drinking in the imperial court when Emperor Qianlong held celebration ceremonies, this was a piece of great jade artwork imitating the style of Hindustan jade.

show that making the jade boulder involved many thousands of jade craftsmen and cost tens of thousands of taels of silver. The creation of such a peerless, precious artwork is testament to the power and wisdom of the Chinese nation. Facing the unparalleled jade boulder, people cannot help but ask how the jade was extracted from the Mileta Mountain and transported to Beijing. Studies show the jade material was originally buried at the top of the Mileta Mountain, and then dug out after removing the stone that covered the jade. Then jade excavators tied the massive boulder with rope and gradually lowered it down the mountainside. To facilitate transport, a big cart was specially made, pulled by dozens of horses and pushed by hundreds of people. It took more than three years to move the jade to Beijing, and during the long journey, the transporters opened roads when coming to mountains, built bridges when encountering rivers and paved ways by pouring water to make it freeze into ice in the winter. After finally arriving in Beijing, they further transported the jade by ship to Yangzhou via the Grand Beijing-Hangzhou Canal for processing. The actual detail of the processing is unknown today except the rough procedures. A wooden model was first made, and a movable shelf was built around the boulder in the process of carving. Scores of jade workers worked day and night on a rotation basis, gradually carving the jade based on the model. The jade boulder was so successful that it is reputed to be one of the wonders of Chinese jade history.

The period of Emperor Qianlong's reign in the Qing Dynasty saw the artistic peak of Chinese jade. At the same time, a kind of foreign jade ware suddenly flourished and gained popularity in the imperial court, which exerted great influence upon jade ware in both the court and society. This was Hindustan jade ware that was highly praised and cherished by Emperor Qianlong. Hindustan jade had a strong Islamic style that was most characterized by its thinness and high transparency. Mostly made of grey and white Hotan jade produced in Xinjiang, Hindustan jade was usually designed for practical use, and included such items as plates, cups, bowls and kettles. Most of the designs featured flowers, fruits and leaves, and some were animal shapes. Hindustan jade was usually carved with the bas-relief technique that was extremely refined and left no tool marks. Meanwhile, thin gold or silver thread, glass or precious stones were often embedded on the jade surface to highlight a sense of dignity. Under the authority of Emperor Qianlong, the jade production department under the Imperial Household Department set up a workshop specializing in duplicating Hindustan jade.

The times of prosperity during the reigns of emperors Kangxi, Yongzheng and Qianlong witnessed another collecting frenzy. Antique jade that first appeared in the Song Dynasty was in extraordinarily high demand at this time. There were many reasons for the popularity of antique jade in the Qing Dynasty: first, it reflected the personal preference of the emperors; second, since the Ming and Qing dynasties there had been great nostalgia for the past which brought ancient styles back in to fashion. As the people in the Qing Dynasty admired antiques and loved the original color of jade materials, they sometimes would purposely heat the jade to produce a yellow layer on the surface if the jade did not have such a color, which showed their strong interest in the ingenious, graduated color typical of antique jade. The practice of bringing out the surface color has a far-reaching influence even today and shows a trend of increasing popularity.

The introduction of jadeite ware was a great event in Qing Dynasty jade history. Jadeite ware was extremely expensive because this stone was not found in China. Since it first came to China through Burma in the eighteenth century, jadeite was greatly cherished and loved by people both in the court and society, as it was fine, tough, crystal-like, elegant and mysterious. Emerald-green jadeite ware, including those used for ornaments, decoration, and in writing and daily life, was fairly outstanding among the jade ware in the late Qing Dynasty. The Empress Dowager Cixi (1835–1908) was particularly fond of emerald-green jadeite, and jadeite ware of various kinds could be seen everywhere in the Palace of Eternal Spring where she lived. She used emerald-green jadeite-covered bowls to drink tea and jadeite chopsticks during meals, inserted jadeite hairpins in her hair, wore jadeite rings on her fingers and often held an emerald-green jadeite cabbage in hands to play with. She called emerald-green jadeite "royal

Emerald-green jadeite cabbage, Qing Dynasty
Jade craftsmen carved out an emerald cabbage using the green and white colors of the raw emerald-green jadeite. It was one of the most outstanding emerald artworks of the Qing Dynasty

jade." It is said that Empress Dowager Cixi had a jewelry room in the Summer Palace, where there was a square-shaped sandalwood cabinet that accommodated glass boxes of different sizes. These delicate boxes wrapped with embroidered silk were filled with various kinds of precious jewelry, among which she loved a pair of emerald-green jadeite watermelons the most. The green, red and black colors of jadeite were ingeniously used in the watermelons. It is said that even the green-black stripes on the watermelon peel, black seeds and red flesh inside the watermelon could be seen clearly, which showed both the beauty of nature and superb craftsmanship of jade artisans.

Empress Dowager Cixi not only collected a vast amount of emerald-green jadeite in her lifetime, but had an amazing number of emerald-green jadeite pieces buried with her when she died. As was later revealed by the Qing Dynasty royal families, in the tomb of Cixi, the two watermelons mentioned above were placed beside her feet; in addition, there were four emerald-green jadeite melons, two had white peel, yellow seeds, and pink flesh, and two had green peel, white seeds, and yellow flesh. There was also a realistic emerald-green jadeite lotus leaf placed at her head, and another twenty-seven jadeite Buddhas, ten emerald-green jadeite peaches and two jadeite cabbages, green outside and white inside, each with a green cricket sitting on it. Cixi inaugurated a new phase of auspicious emerald-green jadeite in Chinese jade history with her efforts, the impact of which has lasted until today.

The splendid jade ware of the Qing Dynasty provided a fitting end to the history of traditional Chinese jade. The ancient Chinese jade ware that appeared under the guidance of a primitive and obscure sense of beauty underwent an 8,000 year evolution. From its first appearance as simple ornaments, to those serving religion, hierarchy and morals, and finally to a kind of high-level artwork, jade has reflected different cultural phenomena in different historical periods and societal ideologies. The jade artwork from different times with diverse styles jointly composed a splendid song, representing the comprehensive 8,000-year-old jade culture of the Chinese nation.

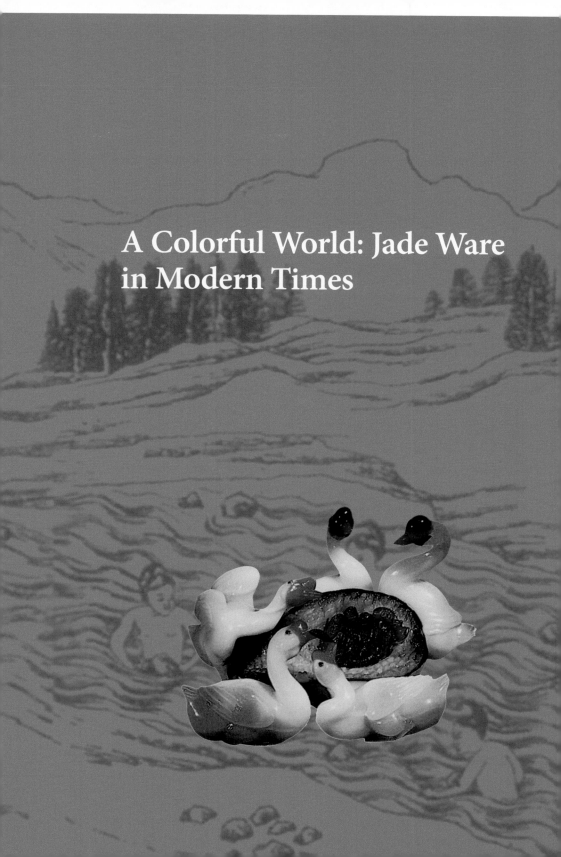

A Colorful World: Jade Ware in Modern Times

C olorful Chinese jade ware is more than the essence of art, or a witness to Chinese history; it represents emotional bonds linking all Chinese people. The evolution of jade ware not only serves as a witness to the dramatic historic changes and reflects the pursuit of the Chinese nation, but also maintains the Chinese people's interest in jade and has become the material carrier of contemporary affection for traditional culture and national spirit.

With the fall of the old China from the end of the nineteenth century to the early twentieth century, jade art, like other art forms, was seriously damaged. But with the rapid recovery and development of the national economy after the founding of the New China in 1949, jade ware came back to life as a branch of Chinese art, and Chinese jade culture shone once more.

Since the 1950s, jade ware workshops have been established in Beijing, Yangzhou, Suzhou, Shanghai, Guangzhou, Tianjin, Nanjing, Gansu, Henan, Liaoning and Xinjiang, and hundreds of jade artists have received great attention and respect from the State and society alike. Based on the different styles of jade design and manufacturing, contemporary Chinese jade ware falls into four genres: the "Northern Genre," "Yangzhou Genre," "Shanghai Genre" and "Southern Genre." The Northern Genre refers to the style of jade-carving masters in such northern areas as Beijing and Liaoning, which featured seriousness and elegance. Artists from this area include Pan Bingheng, famous for carving group figures and thin jade wares, Liu Deying who was very good at carving flowers with round carving techniques, and He Rong, known for round carvings of Buddha and ancient beauties. The Yangzhou Genre referred to the unique techniques adopted by jade artists in Yangzhou, which highlighted fixed procedures and boasted exquisite workmanship. The jade ware, pretty and lively, revealed classic beauty and the representatives were huge jade carvings and *shanzi* carving. Some of them have

The "five geese with ingenious color" made by Wang Shusen, a senior craftsman in Beijing.

even been permanently collected by the State as precious works. The Shanghai Genre was the style of jade artists in the city of Shanghai, and mainly included exquisitely carved antique-style containers and vividly carved figures and animals. The Southern Genre referred to the jade-carving style in the Guangzhou area and was unique in enchasing techniques, as well as carvings on multi-layered balls and high-level emerald-green jadeite ornaments.

The "Five geese with ingenious color" is one of the representative works of Wang Shusen (1917–1989), a master of modern jade ware. A piece of agate with multiple colors was cleverly carved into an image of five geese pecking at food. The geese stand, walk or lie around the food pot, eating, watching and cackling. They have different poses and look extremely lifelike. What surprises us most are that the colors of every part of the geese's bodies and food pot are based on natural colors, which are appropriate and natural. The feathers are grey, the beaks are red, the eyes are black, the food pot is grey-white and the feed is yellow and black. It is easy to imagine how difficult it was to carve a piece of jade ware with such complicated shapes and rich colors. Wang Shusen had successfully carved five vivid-looking geese, both male and female, on a piece of jade that is only four inches long, so it is no wonder the piece of artwork is reputed as a great representative combining superb craftsmanship and an innovative use of colors.

With improvement at scientific and technological levels, and changes in aesthetic concepts, new developments have occurred in raw materials used to make jade ware in modern times. Those often used include Hotan jade, emerald-green jadeite, Xiuyan jade, Dushan jade, Lantian jade, lapis lazuli, turquoise, malachite, agate, crystal, colored glaze, amber and coral, among which Hotan jade and emerald-green jadeite are the most loved.

Among the symbols of Chinese jade culture, Hotan jade ware has grown in popularity in recent years. The prosperity of the traditional places of jade and the rise of emerging markets pushed for the progress of Hotan jade ware, and Hotan jade artwork made in Shanghai, integrating exquisite carving techniques and novel meanings, have brought Chinese jade culture to another peak.

Emerald-green jadeite is mainly used in ornaments. Chinese people love the green color, believing it represents the earth

A model displaying jade ornaments.

and life. The emerald green and its fine, transparent texture are in perfect harmony with the skin color of the Chinese people, and it appears natural and calming. It is also appropriate to use emerald-green jadeite for decoration or as a gift. This not only makes the environment more beautiful, but can also embody people's good wishes through the jades' auspicious implications.

Modern jade ware has retained most of the categories and shapes of traditional Chinese jade ware, but now boasts much richer categories with functions that are quite different from ancient ones and incorporate many innovations. Nowadays, jade ware mainly falls into five categories:

i) Containers, stoves and bottles. Dominated by those with traditional Chinese shapes and patterns, they have shapes intended to simulate antique jade, ceramics and bronzes, and integrate innovations based on traditional features, so they are called "innovative antique jade ware." They include three-feet stoves, multi-layered pagodas, vases, incense burners, cups, tripods, bowls, dishes and boxes.

ii) Jades with auspicious designs of traditional figures, including Buddha and characters in dramas and folktales. In images dominated by figures, there are also hills, stones, boats, gardens, flowers, birds and so on. They are mainly designed to show vivid and realist effects.

iii) Jades with flower and bird patterns. The flowers typically include peonies, China roses, orchids, asphodels and chrysanthemums. Birds include phoenixes, peacocks, cranes, mandarin ducks, chicks, and ducks. The jade ware is designed to display crystal and delicate effects.

iv) Jades with images of beasts that are mostly mythical – dragons, hornless dragons and kylins –as well as lions, tigers, horses and deer. The renderings tend to be realistic or based on traditional ancient animals, and highlight ferocious images and mysterious effects.

v) Miscellaneous. These include a wide range of jade ware, such as tools used in writing like brush racks, paperweights, water bowls and jade ink stones; ornamental jade such as chain beads and bracelets; jade weapons like knives, spears, swords and halberds; antique ritual jade like *gui, zhang, bi, cong, hu* and *huang*; jade used in daily life such as bowls, plates, cups and

Modern jade-making process.

pillows; commemorative jade such as medals and conference gifts. Most of this jade ware is small with a simple and plain style.

Modern jade artifacts with multiple purposes are not only high quality artwork that satisfy people's artistic needs and refine human minds, but also conversions of wealth or currency that represent investment opportunities. They are not only used to show off social status, cultural taste and wealth, but are also a medium for cultural exchanges among counties and precious gifts; they are not only carriers of spiritual wealth, but also spiritual sustenance for humans who pursue happy marriages, good health, longevity and good luck.

Today, jade-ware making has changed greatly with scientific and cultural progress. Different genres of jade ware have made constant innovations by learning from each other and absorbing the strengths of ancient art and Western art. Besides the round carving technique, the skill of combining relief and high relief appeared and openwork, enchasing, carving using ingenious color and embedding techniques were further developed. New techniques and tools were invented one after another – from the jade carving machine invented in the 1960s that replaced the traditional *shuideng*, to the improved high-speed jade carving machine in the 1970s, to the industrial soft shaft used to carve large-sized jade ware, ultrasonic drilling tools and techniques that can finish drilling in minutes, sand-blasting techniques adopted to paint patterns and characters on jade surfaces, as well as "bowl set machines," "hollowing-out machines" and other specially designed modern machines – showing the dramatic progress made in jade ware techniques. The latest jade-making techniques most recently played a big part in the Beijing Olympic Games.

The twenty-ninth Summer Olympic Games were held in Beijing in August 2008. As an important carrier of Beijing culture, jade once again presented the mien of Chinese culture to the world. Two Chinese seals displaying the Beijing Olympic emblem were made of Hotan jade produced in Xinjiang. One of the seals was presented to the Olympic Museum in Lausanne, Switzerland for its permanent collection, and the other is in Beijing's Capital Museum. The Olympic emblem seal, with its main design based on the "Seal of Emperor Huangdi," the most outstanding of the twenty-five seals from the Qing Dynasty collected in the Beijing Palace Museum, has multiple meanings as defined in jade culture: i) Benevolence. Jade's soft sheen represents the Olympic spirit's generosity and comprehensiveness; ii) Wisdom. Jade represents the enterprising spirit, innovation and progress of the Olympics; iii) Courage. The unyielding character of jade implies the "faster, higher, stronger" spirit advocated by the Olympics; iv) Purity. Jade is clear and this symbolizes the noble and pure Olympic spirit. The gold, silver, and bronze medals awarded to athletes at the 2008 Olympic Games were also embedded with white,

The Beijing 2008 Olympic emblem made of Hotan jade.

grey-white, and grey jade and thus were unique and precious. In addition, the music played at the award ceremonies included the sounds made by gold and jade instruments. The Chinese people cheered for the Olympic athletes with this beautiful music to show their great respect. A perfect integration of Chinese jade culture gave the Olympics a strong Chinese flavor and oriental style, and embodied the hospitality of the Chinese nation. It not only demonstrated the warm welcome extended by the Chinese to guests from around the world, but also implied the sincere blessings of the Chinese for people the world over. At this time, ancient Chinese jade culture was injected with new meaning and blossomed again.

CHINESE JADE

During its 8,000-year evolution, Chinese jade ware has been apotheosized and used by rulers, interpreted and beautified by the rules of etiquette, and studied and appreciated by experts, turned from common beautiful stones into something mysterious with super natural powers, marked with signs of religion, politics, morals and values, and thus became the spiritual sustenance of the Chinese. Chinese jade ware is the precious treasure of the Chinese nation and an outstanding representative in the art world. Its history constitutes an epic that records the artistic creativity and indomitable spirit of the Chinese nation and inspires the Chinese people of today to strive unceasingly for greatness.

Appendix
Chronological Table of the Chinese Dynasties

The Paleolithic Period	c.1,700,000–10,000 years ago
The Neolithic Period	c. 10,000–4,000 years ago
Xia Dynasty	2070–1600 BC
Shang Dynasty	1600–1046 BC
Western Zhou Dynasty	1046–771 BC
Spring and Autumn Period	770–476 BC
Warring States Period	475–221 BC
Qin Dynasty	221–206 BC
Western Han Dynasty	206 BC–AD 25
Eastern Han Dynasty	25–220
Three Kingdoms	220–280
Western Jin Dynasty	265–317
Eastern Jin Dynasty	317–420
Northern and Southern Dynasties	420–589
Sui Dynasty	581–618
Tang Dynasty	618–907
Five Dynasties	907–960
Northern Song Dynasty	960–1127
Southern Song Dynasty	1127–1276
Yuan Dynasty	1276–1368
Ming Dynasty	1368–1644
Qing Dynasty	1644–1911
Republic of China	1912–1949
People's Republic of China	Founded in 1949